Harry & Meghan

Vol. 1: Rocking the Monarchy, Settling in California & How Dare They Be Happy

Courtney Hargrove

One Moment Books

Published by ONE MOMENT BOOKS

For information, address
OneMomentBooks@Outlook.com

Contents

1

At the Gates of Independence

July 2020

Prince Harry guided the Land Rover to a stop at the entrance to a private enclave nestled between the Santa Ynez Mountains and the Pacific Ocean. Only weeks before, he and his wife Meghan, the Duchess of Sussex, had closed on their purchase of a mansion in Montecito, a small community in Santa Barbara County. As their protection officers gained entry through the wrought-iron gate flanked by two modest stone pillars topped with two lantern-style nightlights, Harry read the low-key sign letting visitors know they were at the edge of a private lane.

Harry was, finally, *home*. At the end of the road ahead lay the stunning 7.4-acre property he and the former Meghan Markle had purchased for $14.65 million (leaving them with a mortgage of $9.5 million). Since leaving his native England six months earlier, Harry hadn't felt truly settled. He'd been staying in other people's homes—first, one owned by a friend of music producer David Foster on Vancouver Island in Canada, and then in Tyler Perry's Los Angeles mansion—while doing the work of repatriating, immersing himself in a new culture's norms and practices.

This pavement laid out before him in this moment looked like the road to bliss: there weren't just gates protecting the family from intrusion, but also distance. The road was long and when it branched off, a generous driveway gave the Sussexes still more breathing room from a fascinated public.

Meghan was equally happy to be home, but for different reasons. From the moment she'd landed back in California to stay, she'd been inhaling the scent of familiarity all around her. The smell of the air is different, the environment arid compared to the damp of England. Meghan was at peace. Free. Back to her old self already—independent, driven, in control.

For expatriated Harry, it was less of a calm peace than it was a thrilling adventure. There are small things one needs to know in order to conduct a life in a new country. As wealthy and privileged as he was, Harry was nonetheless an expat who must endure the same level of culture shock his wife had when she moved to England to be with him. Anyone who moves between countries will face exciting newness that collides with the surprising uncertainty of the unfamiliar. Both countries run on the English language, but the vernacular is different, the norms are unique, and the culture clash is real.

There were the little things: a brand-new phone number with an American sequence of digits. Driving on the right. Ice machines at bars (ask for ice in an English pub and prepare to be laughed out the door or have one cube picked up deliberately with tongs and plopped grumpily in your drink). Learning American lemonade is *not* fizzy and *does* contain actual lemons. Harry had only ever lived full-time in the United Kingdom. He'd served valiantly in Afghanistan for ten weeks in 2007, and for another four months in 2012-2013. But as life-changing as those experiences were, it was always temporary. "Captain Harry Wales," as he was fondly known in the British Army, had left active duty years ago and though he had been everywhere outside the UK, he'd *lived* nowhere but England. He'd been reminded during six months in North America that visiting is never the same as *settling.*

He was excited to experience his first bout of Santa Anas, those relentless, melancholic winds whistling down the mountains and whooshing through the canyons. He'd take Archie to see his first whales cruising through Santa Barbara Channel, play with him on the beach, play fetch with the dogs in the surf, have romantic nights under fairy lights in their most private of back yards, away from paparazzi and prying eyes.

The gate opened and Harry gripped the wheel harder as he hit the gas. He, Meghan, and their 1-year-old son Archie Mountbatten-Windsor rode with purpose into the exciting, scary and beautiful unknown of their new life. Meghan laid a flat palm on her belly and felt the warmth of the new life growing inside her. She couldn't wait to tell family and friends once she safely hit the first trimester mark. Meghan was eager to bask in that golden hour when her closest circle could join in her excitement and planning and arguing about names, laughing at the bad ones, fretting over the first and second choices, and living in that brief time just before the world found out and her next baby became subject to public commentary.

Meghan's pregnancy wasn't the only secret she and Harry brought through those gates. So far no one outside their circle even knew about this place. They'd bought the property through a trust and the media hadn't figured it out yet. As Harry drove and pointed out palm trees with Archie, he reveled in the knowledge he was safely ensconced with only those he could trust, if even for a short time.

That *still* wasn't all, though. They carried even bigger secrets with them. Exciting ones, frightening ones, shocking ones and not-so-surprising ones. And while no one knew what was coming next, everyone was watching. It felt as if the world's attention shone even hotter on them now than when they were full-time working royals. They had legions of fans including "sugars" and "stans"—those who would defend Meghan to the death and wouldn't tolerate any suggestion she was not heavenly, perfect and brilliant—and there were detractors, loud and forceful and largely anonymous bots and trolls on social media who seemed to despise the couple yet found time in their busy lives to slam the pair at every turn with racist and cruel taunts, lies and conspiracies. Royal reporters and friends of Kensington and Buckingham palaces guessed and claimed and predicted what was next for the couple. They all had it wrong.

None of them had a clue was coming.

November 2019

His Royal Highness Henry Charles Albert David, Duke of Sussex, left his home country in stages. His road to California was paved with emotional confrontations, tangled family relations, and passive-aggressive leaks presumably by palace courtiers to the British media. By the autumn of 2019, things had become so difficult for Harry and his family that he came to face the fact they all needed a break—a long one. No one outside a few trusted (and not-so-trusted) aides knew how unhappy Harry and Meghan were with their position within the royal family.

As he and Meghan worked to set up a plan for a weeks-long break away from the UK, Harry remained haunted by what he'd learned about his wife's well-being earlier that year. Months before, in January 2019, things had become very dark indeed. What was "supposed" to be a happy time—Meghan was pregnant with her first child and seen out and about glowing and smiling for the cameras—was actually a dangerous period for the couple. It felt like negative forces and a hard wind were swirling around them, trapping them, sapping their power.

The darkness had all but engulfed Meghan on a brisk January day, a time of year when it starts to get dark in England in the afternoon. The couple were scheduled to attend a Cirque du Soleil show called Totem at the iconic Royal Albert Hall in London, and Harry was starting to think about getting ready for the evening. He'd be donning a navy suit and a slate tie and thought about giving his beard a little trim.

Meghan, heavily pregnant, had already selected a dark blue Roland Mouret sequined dress. But she couldn't bring herself to put it on. Her long hair was loose, relaxed, tucked behind her ears. Scraping it back into a neat, classic bun to step out into the world seemed like too much effort that night, too.

Her husband noticed. He'd been watching and listening more than ever since she'd shared her deep feelings of hopelessness and depression living in Windsor.

"Stay home," he pleaded that night. "Skip this one. I can handle it on my own." He had to go. The show would benefit his charity Sentebale, so his missing it would have raised eyebrows.

Instead of the relief she expected upon hearing her husband's well-meaning offer, Meghan felt a ripple of fear. She looked him in the eye. "I'll go."

Harry shook his head, not quite understanding. Meghan explained it simply: "I can't be left alone," she said.

Harry knew what that meant and felt her words like a gut-punch. And so Meghan donned the blue dress along with a bright smile, slipped on one of Princess Diana's bracelets, grabbed her Givenchy clutch and off they went. As cameras flashed and crowds called their names, Meghan shook hands with the cast of the show and smiled gamely as she was supposed to as a representative of the stiff-upper-lip British royal family. That night's images released to the public told a story that almost everyone interpreted incorrectly. Meghan "glowed" when the cameras were on her, and she and Harry were "adorable" and "melted

6

hearts" with their "PDA," as *Harper's Bazaar*, to give just one example, put it.

But if you looked closely, you'd see it. You'd see Harry frowning and fidgeting nervously with his wedding ring in one shot. Another image showing what some labeled "PDA" was actually something else entirely: Harry was draping an arm over Meghan's leg and clutching her hand reassuringly; the light has gone out of her eyes and Harry looks morose.

Later, Meghan would recall the odd feeling of putting on her own show at the theater that night. "Every time those lights went down in that royal box, I was just weeping," she said during a bombshell interview with Oprah in 2021. Her husband "was gripping my hand and it was, 'Okay an intermission's coming, the lights are about to come on, everyone's looking at us again'… and you had to be 'on' again."

She got through that night, but things just got worse after that. The ongoing problem was twofold: first, the media scrutiny and brutal headlines continued to pound her, and second, the glaring fact Meghan felt the royal family did nothing to combat the hammering she was getting. That month alone, headlines and stories targeted her most innocent habits. One of the most absurd was the now-famous Avocado Scandal. The media pounced on a friend's social media post about Meghan serving him avocado toast on silver platters. The *Daily Mail*, which has in the past run supportive stories involving climate change deniers, on this occasion was worried sick about the impact of Meghan's lunch on planet Earth. Describing the friend's social media post, the newspaper story read: "'The consummate hostess,' he enthused. Well, perhaps not so much. The campaigning duchess may be passionate when it comes to racial equality and female empowerment, but for someone who wants to save the planet, she's committed something of a faux pas with avocados.

"For all their health benefits and tastiness, the fact is that rampant avocado production in the Third World has been linked with water shortages, human rights abuses, illegal deforestation, ecosystem destruction and general environmental devastation."

Rampant avocado production.

It was almost comical in its absurdity, and Meghan herself commented wryly, "That's one loaded piece of toast!"

Even pettier—and in keeping with the hypocritical coverage of the new American princess—were the headlines about Meghan touching her baby bump as she awaited the birth of her first child. Pregnancy was new to her, and she seemed to find comfort in cradling her tummy. Ah, but that was not a good look, the British press proclaimed. "Why can't Meghan Markle keep her hands off her bump?....Is it pride, vanity, acting—or a new-age bonding technique?" read one headline.

That story ran in January of 2019, a year or so after Kate Middleton had given birth to Prince Louis, when the same newspaper ran a touching headline about the mum-to-be: "Not long to go! Pregnant Kate tenderly cradles her baby bump while wrapping up her royal duties ahead of maternity leave." It continued to be one rule for the new, biracial woman, and another for the quiet, compliant, white English rose. (Note from the future: Even being called out publicly for this disparate treatment, the *Mail* learned nothing—or consciously chose to double down. It's hard to say. But on June 6, 2021, the *Daily Mail* ran a photo of Princess Beatrice out and about. Headline: "Blooming lovely! Princess Beatrice looks glamorous in green as she cradles her burgeoning baby bump while enjoying a sunny day out…").

Meghan kept smiling in public. But she wasn't OK—at all. "I was really ashamed to say it at the time and ashamed to have to admit it to Harry, especially because I know how much loss he's suffered. But I knew that if I didn't say it, that I would do it," Meghan would later tell Oprah, making the startling admission she'd wanted to hurt herself. "I just didn't want to be alive anymore, and that was a very clear and real and frightening constant thought."

At the time, Meghan says she asked for help from those who run the royal family, but was rebuffed because it might reflect badly on The Firm, as the palaces are some-times colloquially referred to. Still, the suicidal thoughts persisted. "I thought it would have solved everything for everyone," Meghan said later.

That made some sense considering how egregious the harm allegedly done to Meghan that year, and the alleged conversations that went on within the family about her son who was due in a matter of months. While she was pregnant, Meghan and Harry say, the color of their unborn baby's skin was discussed by a certain royal family member or members. How dark the boy's might or might not be. What this precious life might look like standing next to a family full of pasty-faced inbreds. It was a new low and though the royals didn't admit to it—in fact sour-faced William denied they were in any way "a racist family"—at the very least Meghan's home country, deep in a reckoning with its own persistent racism, largely seemed to believe her and Harry.

That gloomy winter, Harry saw the looming disaster. He listened. He learned about unconscious bias and knew there was what he called a "race element" to the media and social media attacks, and he waited and hoped and prodded his very powerful family to intervene and speak out for his wife. He was particularly saddened and angry to know that some seventy members of Parliament slammed the "colonial undertones" of so many headlines about Meghan, but Harry's own family stayed silent. "That hurts," he admitted.

It was time to get Meghan away from the toxicity before something terrible happened.

It was viewed initially as a weeks-long holiday break. That November the family retreated to Vancouver Island, a moody, idyllic property at the edge of the Pacific ocean where it was warm enough to grow olives and lemon trees.

Meghan traveled ahead to Canada with Archie. Harry stayed to wrap things up as best he could with the royal family. When he finally left, the world was given a glimpse of his arrival on new ground, captured in photos of him

10

stepping off the plane and preparing to reunite with Meghan and Archie. He wore a blue beanie, a fleece, and a grin with sparkling eyes that said, *Honey, I'm home.*

Of course, they weren't home—not yet. But they were safe at their new launch pad, free and clear and with the world as their oyster. They'd secured a temporary property with the help of legendary music producer David Foster, who hails from Victoria, British Columbia's capital city, a stone's throw from North Saanich. Foster first met Harry and Meghan in London in 2018 and says he was "immediately...drawn to them" and eager to help them find a safe retreat.

It was another testament to the stark dichotomy between the people who actually met the couple and those who never knew them but continued their sniper fire from the shadows. Said Foster, "I felt honoured that I was able to help Meghan there, because I'm a Canadian and we're a Commonwealth country, we're the Crown's. It's important to us, so I grew up with that kind of sentiment. I was really happy to be able to help them find a respite just to take a little time off."

The connection to Foster was the performer Katharine McPhee, newly married to the producer. She and Meghan did musical theatre together as teenagers while they lived in Los Angeles. In January 2019, Katharine posted an old pic of them on her Instagram, which showed the two in heavy makeup grinning at a performance. "Meghan and I did musicals together as kids. She grew up to be the Duchess of Sussex and I grew up to star on the West End, so same life if you ask me. #TBT."

So much was beautiful about that time in their lives. Meghan, Harry and Archie woke up to ocean views and glorious nature around them, and they could *breathe*. Meghan began to feel better slowly, day by day, and her outdoor jaunts over expansive Canadian wilderness with her two men did her good, as did regular visits from her mom, Los Angeles-based Doria Ragland.

But before long, things got hard again. The media found them, and the Sussexes' security concerns instantly spiked. Still, they were safe under the watchful eye of Metropolitan Police protection officers who'd traveled with them from London. As the world's attention once again turned to the couple, Buckingham Palace released a statement: "The Duke of Sussex has been a frequent visitor to Canada over many years, and it was also home to The Duchess for seven years before she became a member of the Royal Family. They are enjoying sharing the warmth of the Canadian people and the beauty of the landscape with their young son."

Just before Christmas, Prime Minster Justin Trudeau Tweeted a welcome to the family. "Prince Harry, Meghan, and Archie, we're all wishing you a quiet and blessed stay in Canada. You're among friends, and always welcome here," he wrote.

They were OK for awhile. Meghan and Harry had private beaches to throw sticks for the dogs, moody winter days with bracing ocean breezes, visits from grandma

Doria, and date nights at the Deep Cove Chalet restaurant. Meghan cooked, as she loves doing, and the little family had fun nights using the pizza oven afforded by the luxury property.

"Meghan takes a walk with Archie every single day through the woods," *Us Weekly* reported. "She either pushes him in a stroller through the paved trails through the public woods by their home or straps him on and walks the more rustic routes. The walks usually last around an hour or two, but she takes them daily." She is "very kind to the locals she meets while hiking," stopping to chat with people about parenting and the weather. "She's all around pleasant to strangers," the magazine reported. "She is telling friends that she is so happy to be out in nature and [in] their secluded area."

Instead of Pilates in Kensington or mommy and me-type classes in Windsor near their home at Frogmore Cottage, the duchess took in the grandeur of nature surrounding them, taking advantage of all the beauty Canada had to offer. Yet in some ways, the more things changed for Meghan the more they stayed the same. She was free and she was back on familiar ground in her beloved Canada. But she remained under scrutiny, such as one day when she committed the grave offense of taking a walk with her baby son and dogs and was slammed for carrying Archie awkwardly or dangerously, as some wrote online. Furthermore, hackles were raised when it was noted she was accompanied by a royal protection officer *and* a Canadian Mountie, which prompted Canadian outcry against having to cover the cost of royal protection. It was the walk in the park that turned into an international incident.

Meghan also kept working, hopping on a seaplane to visit charities who needed her attention, always with an eye on achieving social justice.

At the time, those outside their inner circle didn't know the full extent of what was coming with their split from the monarchy.

This part of Canada, whose cultural ethos professes great discretion and yawns at celebrity, nonetheless catalogued their moves as much as possible. The famous couple wasn't *quite* famous enough, though, to entice a local restaurant to host them on one particularly busy night. The exclusive Deep Cove Chalet restaurant and winery is hard even for the wealthiest residents to get into, and the property has signage warning against looky-loos and uninvited guests. When Harry and Meghan attempted to make reservations on a busy Canadian holiday, they were told the restaurant was full. There were no strings to pull—it was a firm *Not this time, but we hope to see you in the future* kind of response.

The *Vancouver Sun* talked to Bev Koffel, who owns the Deep Cove Chalet with her husband chef Pierre Koffel, and said she'd met with their security guards at the fine-dining restaurant on the waterfront in North Saanich. "'They said, 'How did you figure out who we were?' And I said, 'It wasn't too hard,'" she explained.

Her husband turned them down partly due to over-crowding by customers who had made reservations early, but also because of the difficulty accommodating the couple's robust security team. It was simply too busy a time.

As Christmas drew closer, local officials were bracing for the possible security concerns and privacy issues of the new royal residents. The *Toronto Star* obtained emails discussing about their stay in North Saanich, in which Mayor Geoff Orr showed a careful approach to the couple and their safety: "Unfortunate that the media has been made aware their decision to spend Christmas in these parts," he wrote at 10 p.m. Christmas Eve. "I hope that they are still able to enjoy their time here and maintain some sense of privacy."

Even so, the holiday season had moments of pure peace for the couple. They sent out their first Christmas card as a family of three, taken by Meghan's close friend Janina Gavankar. On New Year's Eve, they shared a roundup video that included a revealing photo of Harry and Archie, taken by Meghan. The grinning boy was bundled up in a brown jacket, grey wool hat with pom-poms and little UGG boots.

It didn't take long for things to get ugly again. Gavankar was compelled to speak out for her friends, and against the British media, after claims of photoshopping the image she took for the Christmas card were wrongly reported by certain tabloid publications.

"Proud to have taken the Christmas photo for one of my best friends and her family," Gavankar wrote on Instagram, along with the image she personally produced. "Here's the original that was sent out (cropped to fit IG)....and to The Mail, I see your campaign against my friend continues. Nice photoshop of my non-photoshopped image. Now may we all get back to the spirit of Christmas and not the spirit of maliciousness."

2

Time to Go

Harry and Meghan looked at one another across the kitchen table. They sometimes met up in the sunny kitchen, setting up their laptops to work together while Archie was otherwise occupied. The pair had one last exchange about a move that would change everything, that once made could not be taken: *Are we sure?*

They were *sure*. And so was posted a historic manifesto that would rock the British monarchy and make global news.

Indeed, it hadn't been all hiking and homemade pizza during their time on Vancouver Island. They'd taken the time and space to iron out exactly how they wanted to disentangle from royal duties, life in the UK, and from Harry's family. They believed their ideas would allow for a smooth transition and good feelings all around, and that their post was a clear way forward for all.

They couldn't have been more wrong.

The now-famous January 8, 2020 Instagram post allowed the couple to share their truth directly with the public without layers of courtiers, advisors and even family members skewing or filtering it. The statement read in full:

After many months of reflection and internal discussions, we have chosen to make a transition this year in starting to carve out a progressive new role within this institution. We intend to step back as 'senior' members of the Royal Family and work to become financially independent, while continuing to fully support Her Majesty The Queen. It is with your encouragement, particularly over the last few years, that we feel prepared to make this adjustment.

We now plan to balance our time between the United Kingdom and North America, continuing to honour our duty to The Queen, the Commonwealth, and our patronages. This geographic balance will enable us to raise our son with an appreciation for the royal tradition into which he was born, while also providing our family with the space to focus on the next chapter, including the launch of our new charitable entity. We look forward to sharing the full details of this exciting next step in due course, as we continue to collaborate with Her Majesty The Queen, The Prince of Wales, The Duke of Cambridge and all relevant parties. Until then, please accept our deepest thanks for your continued support. - The Duke and Duchess of Sussex

This statement meant to show optimism and share early plans was viewed by the monarchy as a grenade lobbed at Buckingham Palace. It infuriated senior royals and top aides, who said they were blindsided by the very public move and balked at the way the Sussexes went around the Queen—it was beyond unseemly.

The royals scrambled to organize a summit at the Queen's Sandringham estate. Future kings Charles and William attended, and as discussions heated up, it quickly became obvious that having Harry "step back" halfway was not going to work—on any level.

The Queen waited long, nail-biting days before finally putting out a statement of her own on January 13:

Although we would have preferred them to remain full-time working Members of the Royal Family, we respect and understand their wish to live a more independent life as a family while remaining a valued part of my family.

Harry and Meghan have made clear that they do not want to be reliant on public funds in their new lives.

It has therefore been agreed that there will be a period of transition in which the Sussexes will spend time in Canada and the UK. These are complex matters for my family to resolve, and there is some more work to be done, but I have asked for final decisions to be reached in the coming days.

And so it was done. Things moved at warp speed after that, as no one seemed to want to drag out the family split. Exactly ten days after the Sussex's Instagram bombshell, the Queen put out another statement:

Following many months of conversations and more recent discussions, I am pleased that together we have found a constructive and supportive way forward for my grandson and his family.

Harry, Meghan and Archie will always be much loved members of my family.

I recognise the challenges they have experienced as a result of intense scrutiny over the last two years and support their wish for a more independent life.

I want to thank them for all their dedicated work across this country, the Commonwealth and beyond, and am particularly proud of how Meghan has so quickly become one of the family.

It is my whole family's hope that today's agreement allows them to start building a happy and peaceful new life.

Unfortunately, as kind and conciliatory as the tone was in that statement, as well as the fact the queen left the door open in case they wanted to come back within a year, the move came with an upsetting condition: Harry, a proud and true member of the British Army for years, would be stripped of those titles he'd been awarded as a royal—such positions as Captain General of the Royal Marines and Honorary Air Force and Commandant of the Royal Air Force would be taken away, a particularly cold move that broke his heart.

He decided to speak out. He was back in England on January 20, 2020 for an event. His speech at a dinner for Sentebale, the cause so dear to his heart, was emotional, frank and sincere: *I must say that I can only imagine what you may have heard, or perhaps read, over the past few weeks. So, I want you to hear the truth from me. As much as I can share, not as a prince or a duke, but as Harry, the same person that many of you have watched grow up over the past 35 years, but now with a clearer perspective.*

The U.K. is my home and a place that I love. That will never change. I have grown up feeling supported by so many of you, and I watched as you welcomed Meghan with open arms, as you saw the love and happiness that I had hoped for all my life. Finally, the second son of Diana got hitched, hooray!

I also know that you've come to know me well enough over all these years to trust that the woman I chose as my wife upholds the same values as I do, and she does. And she's the same woman I fell in love with. We both do everything we can to fly the flag and carry out our roles for this country with pride. Once Meghan and I were married, we were excited, we were hopeful and we were here to serve. For those reasons, it brings me great sadness that it has come to this. The decision that I have made for my wife and I to step back is not one I made lightly. It was so many months of talks after so many years of challenges. And I know I haven't always gotten it right, but as far as this goes, there really was no other option.

I will always have the utmost respect for my grandmother, my commander in chief, and I'm incredibly grateful to her and the rest of my family for the support they have shown Meghan and I over the last few months. I will continue to be the same man who holds his country dear and dedicates his life to supporting the causes, charities and military communities that are so important to me. Together, you have given me an education about living, and this role has taught me more about what is right and just than I could ever have imagined. We are taking a leap of faith, so thank you for giving me the courage to take this next step.

What I want to make clear is, we're not walking away, and we certainly aren't walking away from you. Our hope was to continue serving the queen, the commonwealth and my military associations, but without public funding. Unfortunately, that wasn't possible. I've accepted this knowing it doesn't change who I am or how committed I am, but I hope it helps you understand what it had come to, that I would step my family back from all I have ever known to take a step forward into what I hope can be a more peaceful life.

I was born into this life, and it is a great honor to serve my country and the queen. When I lost my mum 23 years ago, you took me under your wing. You looked after me for so long, but the media is a powerful force. And my hope is one day our collective support for each other can be more powerful, because this is so much bigger than just us. It has been our privilege to serve you, and we will continue to lead a life of service. So in that respect, nothing changes. It has also been a privilege to meet so many of you, and to feel your excitement for our son, Archie, who saw snow for the first time the other day and thought it was bloody brilliant.

It was done. Harry called Meghan, who was still back in Canada with Archie, and they began to process the exciting new freedom as well as the pain of loss, two things that are so often entangled with any life change. Even the most positive ones.

Far from feeling scared to be disconnected from the Sovereign Grant—money the British taxpayers give to support the royal family—Harry felt exhilarated. The strings attached to accepting those finances were a constricting harness that made him feel like a marionette at times, dancing to the rhythm of the British press and making him feel as if he owed the world a piece of himself he wasn't comfortable giving.

The prospect of making a living on his own was more exciting than frightening; Harry knew what a powerful, inventive team he and Meghan made, how creative they were, how fastidious and hard-working. They would put their heads together and thrive in their pursuit of an independent income.

Not everyone understood that. At that time, few knew what a fraught and charged ending he was having with his British family. Only later would it be revealed Harry and Meghan didn't abruptly leave town in a strop to live free of responsibility in North America. Rather, they felt they'd made their grievances quite clear to the family and to The Firm for many months, but had been roundly ignored. They felt they'd tried their best to give as much as they could without losing themselves entirely. When they finally made the decision to leave, they felt they'd done their level best to engender a warm and agreeable parting in which they would continue to serve Her Majesty the Queen and the monarchy in a way that felt healthier for all involved.

And so when the final blow came, it hit Harry and Meghan like a ton of gold bricks.

It was much sooner than most knew when Harry got the bad news. First, he said, his family "literally cut me off financially" shortly after announcing their exit from the Royal family. "By this point, courtesy of the *Daily Mail*, the world knew our exact location," he would add.

This made protection for the family even more vital. The Sussexes' annual security costs have been estimated to be at least $2 to $3 million, according to *Forbes*. But all of the sudden, with no warning, the British royal family told Harry he would no longer receive their protection. Their royal security detail would be cut off—even as they were in the process of finalizing their exit, with the intention of continuing to serve the queen, the prince claimed.

"Their justification was a change in status," Harry explained. "To which I pushed back and said, is there a change in threat or risk?"

Harry wasn't asking for a dime to pay for housing or food or vacations. But he did expect that the danger he was born into would be mitigated by his extraordinarily wealthy relatives, just as it was for other senior royals in line for the throne.

"I was born into this position, I inherited the risk," Harry said. He could hardly believe his young family was left twisting in the wind, a vulnerable and easy target. His pleas fell on deaf hears, Harry said, and his father wouldn't even take his calls.

In light of that, Meghan took pen to paper and wrote plainly of her fears. She begged The Firm, the Queen, the palaces, Charles: She asked them all "to keep my husband safe." Meghan says that she wrote, "Please, it's very clear the protection of me or Archie is not a priority, I accept that, that is fine — please keep my husband safe...I see the death threats, I see the racist propaganda, please keep him safe, please don't pull his security and announce to the world when he and we are most vulnerable."

According to Prince Harry, there were "obvious signs before we got married that this was going to be really hard," with the Palace allegedly suggesting Meghan should continue acting "because there's not the money to pay for her [security]."

They were left blinking into the sun at the speed with which their protection was whipped away, Harry said.

Meghan was apoplectic. "We haven't created this monster machine around us in terms of clickbait and tabloid fodder," she said. The royal family and The Firm "allowed that to happen, which means our son needs to be safe."

Again, they received no sympathy or redress. When their senior royal status officially ended at the end of March, they would be on their own.

If there was ever any doubt they'd made the right decision in leaving, the events of March 2020 eliminated them. It was time to remove themselves from such insulting public encounters like the one put on show during Commonwealth Day Services at Westminster Abbey. The final and very public show of the inner turmoil among senior royals happened on March 9. Meghan, an American without the societal requirement to affix fashionable pieces to her head for every fancy occasion, reportedly pronounced brightly to her staff as she was getting ready, "The last hat for a while, guys!"

Such levity would quickly be drained from the day, because things were about to get ugly. The icy treatment of Harry and Meghan by their own family was no illusion imagined by a fascinated public—it was very much an authentic and intimate moment of cold dismissal by the likes of William and Kate, according to reporting after the fact. Because Meghan and Harry had eschewed the royals' traditional Sandringham Christmas months before, this would mark the first time William, Kate, Harry and Meghan, otherwise known as the erstwhile Fab Four, had been seen together in months.

Meghan selected a bright green dress by Emilia Wickstead for the occasion, and as her "last hat" she wore a William Chambers fascinator in the same color. She stood out in vivid hues, and many suspected the fashion choice was a purposeful statement to say, *I'm still here, and I'm fine.*

But she wouldn't be showing off her outfit for the main event, which was the very public walk with the Queen. Unlike past years, Harry and Meghan would not be in the procession along with the Queen—they'd been cast out, to Harry's great chagrin. Trying to avoid too many bad feelings, at the very last minute the Cambridges agreed to be seated around the same time as Sophie, Edward, Meghan and Harry. But when William and Kate arrived to take their seats, and an already seated Meghan and Harry smiled up at them, the Cambridges appeared to give them short shrift; they saved their smiles *only* for Sophie and Edward. Meghan beamed as she greeted Kate and William, but it appeared Meghan got nothing in return. She was, on her final official royal engagement possibly for the rest of her life, publicly and coldly snubbed.

There were endless analyses and opinions of what happened, and *Finding Freedom,* the book that those in the know strongly believe was done with the tacit permission of the Sussexes (their friends and coworkers and staff would *not ever* speak out without permission. To do so would guarantee being cast out of their gilded circle, and it wouldn't be worth it by any measure), outlined it this way: William arrived, nodded to his brother and offered a terse greeting of "Harry"—and ignored Meghan altogether. As they all waited for the Queen to arrive, the Cambridges kept their backs to the Sussexes, "only turning around to chat with Edward and Sophie, who sat behind them…Although Meghan tried to make eye contact with Kate, the duchess barely acknowledged her," the book reports, and adds quotes from a close friend of the Sussexes who said plainly that the Cambridges made a conscious choice "not to be welcoming. It was most unpleasant."

A video clip of that moment went round the world, with fans and non-royal watchers alike fascinated with the display of family discord they normally worked so hard to keep hidden. This time, the British royal family couldn't cloak their growing rift, and the Cambridges in particular did not bother faking warmth.

"Royal Fans Can't Stop Analyzing This Video Of Harry, Meghan, William And Kate," read a *Huffington Post* headline. Other publications wrote of the "snub" and the "cold" way the Sussexes were treated.

That watershed moment of tension had been a long time coming. Reports suggest the genesis of the trouble between the brothers was the now-famous confrontation years before when William reportedly told Harry he was rushing into a serious relationship with Meghan and that he should slow things down; Harry didn't take kindly to those words. (That said, some royal watchers have suggested there is a far more scandalous reason a rift between the brothers cracked open like the San Andreas fault. If readers want to cheat and make an entire affair out of searching for those claims online, they will find that it is not a rosy picture).

Furthermore, according to Robert Lacey's royal biography *Battle of Brothers: William & Harry—The Inside Story of a Family in Tumult*, William made things worse when he attempted to enlist his late mother's younger brother, Charles Spencer, to chime in on the burning-hot relationship. Harry was furious, according to Lacey, who adds that William was partial to his own way of wooing Kate, who he left twisting in the wind for a decade because he "had been auditioning her for a job all those years." Other royal fans, however, wondered if part of the upset could be due to the idea that William possibly felt some jealousy, and that he wasn't feeling the same exciting, all-encompassing fire for his own wife that Harry clearly felt for Meghan. The British press has long posited that longtime friend Jecca Craig could be William's one true love, though only he knows what's truly in his heart. But as royal-friendly stalwart Richard Kay wrote in *The Daily Mail* in 2016, one is left to wonder…

"Many a young man meets a girl he does not marry, but whom he cannot quite get out of his system. Courtship and romance are followed by a life-long affection, together with nagging thoughts of what might have been.

"Some will wonder if these were the emotions stirring deep with Prince William when he abruptly announced that he was flying to Kenya for the Easter weekend, in order to attend the wedding of his old flame Jecca Craig."

Kay goes on to wonder aloud why William attended alone, leaving Kate and the kids back in England, and further mused about what the draw back to Kenya is for the Prince.

Though the palace denied theirs was ever more than friendship between Jecca and William, Kay's kicker hints otherwise: "Perhaps the speculation would have faded more quickly if William had not so often returned to the Lewa Downs conservancy, a wildlife reserve Jecca's father Ian created on the 55,000 acres his family have farmed since 1922."

And so, when Harry—who has dated English roses and well-traveled beauties and gotten the wild partying out of his system with nubile young ladies in ways including a much-publicized and extended Las Vegas party—finally met the One at the exact right time and fell into her like he'd found the other half of his own soul, many were left to wonder if that triggered William. Perhaps William, who Harry believes is "trapped" in his own position in the UK and within the firm, saw a fire and a wholeness he might never get to experience in his daily life, and perhaps he thought he could make himself feel better by pulling his brother back into the more careful and calculated way of conducting romance. Or perhaps not. Only William knows the truth. And maybe Kate. And maybe a few others. Or possibly just William. We can't know for sure.

Anyway, William had a talk with Harry. A serious, big-brother talk that turned out to be ill-advised in which he told his younger brother to "slow down." Which didn't sit well with Harry, who reportedly wondered "whether Wills was really concerned about his personal happiness—or whether he was, once again and as per usual, thinking about the make-up and fortunes of 'the Firm' whose boss he would become one day?"

In any case, the very public snub that day served to fuel more woman-against-woman media coverage and chatter about the two sisters-in-law. To be sure, they are like chalk and cheese, as the Brits like to say. Kate and Megan had vastly different upbringings and chose different roles for their lives. Meghan is an activist and built a career in one of the most competitive professions in the world. Kate did some part-time work and said she worked for her family company Party Pieces, and spent years living in a London flat paid for by someone else waiting for William to propose, thus earning the rather harsh nickname "Waity Katy."

This kind of quiet patience is well-suited to her role within the British royal family. "One of the expectations of Kate is to be seen and not heard. Problem is, sometimes it seems like she's a blank slate that lets you write on her," said a reporter who covered the royals. "She is rewarded and praised for being silent, dutiful and attractive. For those who admire and demand these traits a woman in the year 2021, Kate is the perfect consort. She is a commoner just like Meghan, but as several royal watchers have noted in the past, Meghan is the 'wrong' kind of commoner to please many inside The Firm."

But here's the thing: Meghan has made it clear she will not be drawn into comparisons to, nor will she drag down, her sister-in-law. She went out of her way to call Kate "a good person" during her interview with Oprah, and she also reminded everyone out there that the two women are actually two separate human beings: "I think so much of what I have seen play out is this idea of polarity, where if you love me, you don't have to hate her. And if you love her, you don't need to hate me."

Ain't that the truth. Yet without pitting woman against woman, where are the clicks? Where are the viewers? Where is the ad revenue? Their "feud" continued courtesy of the world's media even with nary a word from either Meghan or Kate about the other. Their relationship is very much a surface one, say reports, and it has by all accounts been fraught with bad feelings all around—just like every family. For Meghan and Kate, there is no need to turn that into a woman-vs.-woman, or, as Meghan put it, "a narrative of a hero and a villain."

Ah, if only that were the truth. There was a "need"— the media needed it, and they refused to release their jaws and drop it. They gripped tighter.

3

A Dash for the Border

Almost as soon as Harry said goodbye to England and royal life in March 2020, the entire world changed on a dime. Everything was upended, uncertainty reigned, unprecedented lockdowns forced entire populations indoors, and people were dying in terror and agony as the COVID-19 pandemic gripped the globe.

Harry knew immediately it was time to say goodbye to Canada now. "The borders are closing, the world knows where we are, it's not safe or secure," he said to Meghan. "We probably need to get out."

Things were indeed shutting down rapidly, and if they stayed put in a location known to the world without their royal protection team, the family could be stuck for an indefinite time in a place where neither one had citizenship. Harry was ready to dip into his inheritance from his mother, but the need didn't arise: A wealthy celebrity stepped in to offer them refuge. The Sussex family packed up and headed to Meghan's home state of California.

They dropped their bags in Beverly Hills. Though never publicly connected to actor, writer and mogul Tyler

Perry, Meghan and Harry were closely connected through mutual friend Oprah Winfrey, and Perry had a vacant 24,000 square foot mansion—and a ready made security team in place to watch over them. With eight bedrooms and twelve bathrooms, there was room for the Sussexes, their staff, and of course mom Doria, who lives in Los Angeles and would be making regular overnight visits.

Perry had not only given them safe haven within its walls in Beverly Ridge Estates nestled in twenty-two acres above the Los Angeles skyline, but also provided his own security team indefinitely to protect the newly independent young family. It was here they would wait out the quarantine while searching for a place would finally feel like home to *both* of them.

As unsettled as they still were, they strove for normalcy for Archie's sake. Almost immediately they were seen out walking the dogs on nearby hiking trails, and even as COVID-19 swept the land they kept up their outreach and charitable work. At risk to themselves, they both donned their masks and delivered food to at-risk people who could face death if they stepped out to risk catching the virus.

This temporary resting place would also be the site of Archie's first birthday. They made this key milestone as special as ever, decorating the deck of a crystalline pool with balloons.

Meghan baked a "smash" cake—also known as baby's first cake, this is a tiny confection meant for one-year-old to feed themselves and cause the expected mess—with strawberries and cream. Archie dove in as expected, to the delight of the young family. With pandemic protocols requiring restraint and great care, Mom Doria wasn't in attendance that day. She saved her visit for a safe, distanced gathering for mother's day—Meghan's second as a mother herself.

Perry's hideout, situated five miles from busy Sunset Boulevard, was meant to be resting spot to give them room to breathe. But almost as soon as they exhaled, the walls began to close in again. Drones flew overhead and hikers on public trails ventured dangerously close. They were side-eyed for erecting privacy screens around the property when the hiking trails were re-opened in May so that anyone walking past—or trying to stare into their home— could do so. In early May, workers were seen installing the screens so the Sussexes weren't so much on show.

The decision to put up barriers hadn't been a hard one. As helicopters circled and drones flew into view and paparazzi were cutting holes in their fence one day, Harry shouted to their protection team over the din, "Where's the safest place? Where do we go?"

He was taking in the stunning view, the crystalline pool, the landscaped grounds—all a perfect playground for a young family to soak up the southern California sun, but for the relentless invaders. The jarring juxtaposition was almost too much to bear.

Security shouted back, "Get inside!"

All the while they were pounding the phones and working their laptops forging a new career as a couple, and individually. They were in talks with the biggest names, talents and companies in the world. It was a matter of survival. As Harry explained their financial situation, "I've got what my mum left me. Without that, we would not have been able to do this." But there was only so much, and now that they had to pay their own security bill, they needed income.

The overtures were relentless—and not easy to sift through. A couple of their profile and historical importance would be receiving more offers from more colorful origins than the average person can imagine. Oligarchs, kings, celebrities, magnates, singers, artists, despots. They have to filter out the dodgy inquires from the downright dangerous, from the useful to the most altruistic. If they accept a home or a private-jet flight or get into a well-paid but murky business deal, who will they owe favors to, and what will they owe? It's a balance and when they accepted a stay at this L.A. home, for example, thought they found it in Tyler Perry, a man who could afford to do a heart-felt favor with no expectation of a thing in return.

This was relatively new for both of them. Harry hadn't ever been allowed to search out or accept so many interesting opportunities while he was a working royal—it was ostensibly unseemly and forbidden to profit off those connections. As for Meghan, she had abruptly entered the stratosphere after life as an actor on an ensemble cable show during which her publicity team worked tirelessly to get her into magazines and publications. Back then, when she was considered "just an actress," by many detractors, her highly paid public relations team were constantly pushing her to national publications as everything from a rising star in acting to a burgeoning, committed lifestyle expert.

One writer who dealt with her team in 2015 explained they got a pitch saying, "She is an extreme foodie. She is a great cook and … she has a major focus on great food and ambiance," read one pitch from her high-powered reps to a prestigious lifestyle site for a home entertaining story they were working on. The publication didn't bite—the editors balked at Meghan's lack of name recognition. Now she was fending them off non-stop.

Their new careers weren't all they had to worry about. Almost as soon as they unpacked their bags at Perry's place it was time to house hunt. Harry sought peace, quiet and neighbors who wouldn't give the Prince and his beautiful bride a second glance.

Meghan was happy to be a short drive from power lunches and roots, home again where her old haunts and stomping grounds embraced her with a welcome familiarity. She'd left as a working actor and activist and returned an influential duchess with a track record of doing good in the world.

For Harry, the noise, smog and traffic of her hometown were a bit much. Even such a sprawling property as the one they were staying in was still not enough to keep away the prying eyes and violation of paparazzi and their ilk who were out to make a living off of invading the growing family's privacy. Harry had always hunted with his family, but now *he* was in the crosshairs of L.A.'s ruthless celebrity game hunters. While Meghan browsed listings for hillside mansions with an infinity pool and sweeping views of the city she loved—after all, the likes of Jennifer Aniston, prized prey for the paparazzi herself, had made it work—Harry was off kilter amid the packed city.

They talked to each other, consulted friends, drove around, did their research. As always, they came up with a solution that suited them both: it was to be Santa Barbara. They started looking for real estate in wine country, a place that also has a thriving polo community, a beach for Archie and the dogs, and sits just 90 miles away from those power lunches and galas Harry and Meghan would need to attend to keep up their profile.

"They were craving a smaller community and a slower pace—Montecito is very mellow, a charming little town and the Santa Barbara [area] offers an ideal lifestyle that they're looking forward to," a source close to the couple told *People* magazine. "They feel like the future holds endless possibility," the source adds. "They can hope to give Archie as normal a life as possible there."

The stunning property was dotted with olive trees and surrounded by citrus groves, had a playground with a covered slide, palm trees, the Santa Ynez Mountains, and sat a short walk to the beach. World-famous stars live or have lived nearby, equally relishing the privacy afforded by wild landscapes and ample fencing. From Oprah to Tom Cruise to Ariana Grande and Gwyneth Paltrow, famous faces are nothing new around Montecito, these long private roads and secluded estates presented a perfect situation.

They were ecstatic, as ecstatic as a family can be in a worsening pandemic with no discernable end, because there was more happy news. Even with the difficult changes going on, the Sussex family had more than a new home to celebrate: Meghan was pregnant with their second child.

Harry had traded timeworn brick castles for southwestern stucco and damp English winters for Santa Ana winds, and he'd never been happier. The nagging feeling from unrest in his extended family notwithstanding, Harry was once and for all *content*—and knew in his bones he'd done the right thing even in light of the severe blowback he'd received. He'd stood tall, faced the headwinds, and held his ground. They'd closed on The 14,563-square-foot home known as "The Chateau" on June 18, and life was good. Meghan was pregnant, feeling great, opportunities for creative content deals were flying at them, and now they had a home.

They moved in that July, and now here he was, pulling into the home he and his wife had bought without Prince Charles's help or grace and favor.

Once again the Sussexes were heading into a honeymoon period—even if they suspected it might be brief—during which no one knew where they were, and they were, once and for all and for a precious moment in time, *free*.

4

Santa Barbara Life

Harry took to the outdoor lifestyle right away. He has a history of traveling to natural beauty all around the world, from Africa to the Caribbean to Scotland, of course, but this was his first time living his day-to-day life in mother nature's California bosom.

"To have outdoor space where I can go for walks with Archie and we go for walks as a family and with the dogs. You know, we go on hikes or go down to the beach, which is so close," Harry told Oprah. "The highlight for me is sticking him on the back of the bicycle in his little baby seat and taking him on bike rides is something which I never was able to do when I was young. I can see him on the back, and he's got his arms out, chatting: 'Palm tree?' House?'"

He had seen the beauty and the cruelty the world has to offer, and as a couple they'd traveled the world. They'd gazed together upon the Northern lights from the frigid shores of Norway in winter and relaxed on the sun-choked plains of Botswana in August. This felt different; *now* he was home. Here he had privacy and freedom to walk among the coolly indifferent Santa Barbara locals, many wealthier and accomplished and famous than either Harry or Meghan. The world changed in a moment. The moment it became undeniable that COVID-19 was a global threat and a pandemic raged around them. He happily swapped brick-and-mortar castles for sand ones.

Santa Barbara is a chic, quaint country town with an urban flair. Hungry, wealthy people have their choice of restaurants including sushi, Mexican, Italian and a steak house. Meghan was drawn, as always, to yoga, of course—but also mommy and baby yoga. She loves reading and collecting books, and there are a few local stores for her to visit if she's in a browsing mood and craving the feel and smell of a new book, that tactile sense you can't get online. Mary Sheldon, who owns a bookstore near the Sussexes and lives within walking distance of their Italian-style villa, has talked about Oprah's love of the store; the uber-interviewer will often call ahead to order books, and pop in to pick them up without any entourage. It is likely Meghan would pop in, too. She centered herself with her beloved yoga, something Harry has taken to since meeting her.

She would also spend a lot of time in the grand kitchen, of which the home's original owner said, "The kitchen is probably one of the coolest rooms in the house. It opens on to the side patio where the pizza oven and outdoor tables are. Living in Montecito, there's a lot of indoor-outdoor lifestyle, so you easily move from decks to indoors. My wife designed the whole kitchen and loved the layout and flow, so she could do her thing while there's a two-year-old hanging on to her shin."

The grounds are their recreational area, a lush expanse waiting to explore with Archie, to show him what he'd never have seen in Britain, citrus trees heavy with ripening lemons turning from green to yellow, ready for Meghan to pluck and bake into a delectable dessert whenever they're in season. When prime orange-picking season came around in spring, Meghan could take her basket, Archie toddling along ahead, and pick the perfect fruit of her own land.

She was, in fact, living life the way she'd once advised others to do.

"Take things with a grain of salt and find balance within your life," she once said in an interview. "On your lunch break, leave to go and get some fresh air. You don't need to make your life your job."

"I have to find that balance for myself, as well," she said. "Between The Tig and my time on set or at home, I have to make the time to throw in a yoga class or walk my dogs or literally just turn it all off and meditate for a minute. I think you have to make time for yourself so that work doesn't become the end-all be-all."

There were no reports that she or her husband worried much about the natural enemies surrounding them. Indeed, the beauty and grandeur of their surroundings are balanced equally by the vast power of mother nature's wrath; when she decides to turn her hand to burying mudslides, inundating tsunamis, and ground-shaking earthquakes, Californians are often in grave danger. The

Ventura Fault is there, newly believed to be a greater risk than previously thought, and City of Santa Barbara's emergency services office has said the city got its tsunami maps in 2009 and officially became a "tsunami-ready" community in 2011. There are human-made hazards in massive wildfires eating up everything in their path. It was only in 2018 that pounding mudslides poured perilously close to the Sussexes' new property. Warned a past owner in a newspaper interview, "We sure as hell didn't think about it [the mudslides] when we were building, but certainly it's something I would be thinking about now."

As it happened for many around the world that pandemic year, the changes kept coming like rogue waves blindsiding expectations of smooth sailing. The Sussexes were no exception. Archie's beloved nanny, a fixture in their lives, raced back home to the UK to be with friends and family as borders were shored up worldwide and a terrifying sense of doom penetrated even the safest spaces.

Try as she might to create a sense of normalcy and security with celebrations and distanced family time, as much as her life appeared to be a fairytale to so many, Meghan was mortal and subject to the same tragedies humanity has endured since our existence.

Around the time Meghan was celebrating her second Mother's Day with Doria, Harry and Archie, she learned she was pregnant with her second child. It was a reason for cautious celebration. The couple glowed and hugged and beamed, and they held on to the promise of better days. They are human, and humans survive on hope no matter where you are; as the late Christopher Reeve once said, "once you choose hope, anything's possible."

Meghan and Harry couldn't help but talk about their future child and started talking about baby names, but they didn't let themselves indulge in a fully formed picture of a family of four. Women in America are culturally guided to be secretive and circumspect in early pregnancy, to delay hope and resist the urge to plan. Harry and Meghan were no exception. Until after that vital first trimester scan, they would keep the news to themselves. They had a lot to distract them, too. They'd filed lawsuits against paparazzi allegedly flying drones over their L.A. home and cutting holes in the fences ringing the property to capture private pictures.

In July, once safely ensconced in their own house, Harry and Meghan filed a harassment lawsuit in L.A. County Superior Court, alleging that paparazzi were flying drones overhead and cutting holes in the fence to photograph their family in the Los Angeles home they'd just vacated. They unpacked.

In the midst of a stressful move, Meghan found time to make an appearance for a cause very close to her heart. She found time to make a video for the U.N. Foundation's virtual 2020 Girl Up Leadership Summit, which offers leadership advice for young girls.

"Continue to believe in yourselves, believe in what makes you unique. And don't be afraid to do what you know is right, even when it's not popular," Meghan said in the video. "Even when it's never been done before. Even if it scares people. And even if it scares you a little.

"Women have always historically gotten a lot of, 'That's not how it's done,' 'Yeah, that's a good idea but we're going to do this instead,'" Meghan continued. "But when do we hear that as women? We hear that in the moments that we challenge the norms. So if that's the case, I say to you, keep challenging. Keep pushing. Make them a little uncomfortable because it's only in that discomfort that we actually create the conditions to reimagine our standards, our policies, and our leadership — to move toward real representation and meaningful influence over the structures of decision-making and power."

Creating a more equitable society will require everyone to join the movement, Meghan said: "I believe we are on the precipice of transformation."

Located on the grounds of what's known as the old Riven Rock estate, the new Sussex property covers some ten acres and boasts sweeping lawns, tiered rose gardens, tall Italian cypress trees, blooming lavender, century-old olive trees, a tennis court, tea house, children's cottage and a pool.

Once they were moved in, Meghan took stock of the sprawling property. There was the playhouse, the guest house, wine cellar, spa with a separate dry and wet sauna, a gym with a stripper pole, game room, arcade, library, movie room, tennis court, rose bushes, the pool, and all those exotic trees Harry would have never seen growing naturally in England.

They brought in casual, weathered wooden garden furniture and tamed the wild foliage framing manicured lawns. The home was warmed with Diptyque candles and bright, cream sofas with pattered pillows of black and grey stripes, and on one Zoom call the world saw some paint samples splotched on the wall in charcoal and dark grey.

But even before the interior designing was nearing its end, even before everything was in its place, Meghan was spending time in the enviable kitchen. One way she shows love and respect in her personal and professional life is through sharing her cooking and baking. Before she left showbusiness and shut down her lifestyle blog The Tig, her publicists were pitching her hard to international media as an "extreme foodie" and discerning gourmand.

She's known to have talent. Before her visit with a farming family in Australia, for example, exhausted in the early stages of pregnancy when she was expecting Archie, she stayed up late peeling overripe bananas and baking them into her special banana cake. As she worried aloud whether there was too much of the fruit in this batch, Harry publicly professed his love of his wife's cake and pronounced, "there can never be too many bananas!"

Meghan would do anything she could to be gracious and generous to the people who would now be living in the family's royal sphere. As she once told a young woman she brought the handmade banana cake to, "If you go to someone's house, you always bring something." Well, she was in the Montecito residents' house now, and it was time to come up with a fitting gesture.

With the kitchen not in full use—how can she find a cake pan when the boxes aren't even fully unpacked yet?—and Meghan mindful of the pandemic and transference of the still poorly understood virus, she ordered presents to be sent to neighbors as sort of reverse-welcome gifts, complete with a hand-signed note. In a different time, there's every chance she would have baked a personal basket of goodies for her new neighbors upon moving to their little enclave, say insiders, but she felt the immediacy of the gesture was better executed using local companies to deliver gifts to introduce the family to locals. It's not confirmed exactly what she and Harry sent, but baked goods, floral arrangements and other gestures have been suggested.

This gesture, while not officially confirmed by the Sussexes' camp, certainly tracks with what we know about the pair, as well as what they have revealed about their concerns of moving to any community to which they know they'll bring unwanted attention.

As heady as those days were, July was a tumultuous month for the young family. They were in talks with various content companies—streaming services, production companies, broadcasters, studios. The size and scope of the deals they were looking for added up to the $100 million range, according to sources who were involved in some of the discussions. They had plenty of help and staff to help them, but with a toddler running around and Meghan drained from early pregnancy, she and Harry had their hands full setting up their new home and arranging their own security team.

But things went from busy and slightly stressful to traumatic in the blink of an eye. On a chaotic, hot July day, Meghan arose, gathered her locks into a ponytail, and began her usual morning routine. She prepared breakfast for the humans and the pets, then made sure to take her own prenatal vitamins and began tidying up.

Archie was awake, so she padded in and lifted him out of his crib. What came next in her own words: "After changing his diaper, I felt a sharp cramp. I dropped to the floor with him in my arms, humming a lullaby to keep us both calm, the cheerful tune a stark contrast to my sense that something was not right," the duchess of Sussex later wrote in a heart-wrenching piece in the *New York Times*. "I knew, as I clutched my firstborn child, that I was losing my second."

Meghan ended up in the hospital, where she stared at the cold, white walls and clung to Harry, watching his "heart break as he tried to hold the shattered pieces of mine."

One saving grace was their new hideaway, which none of the nosy reporters and invasive paparazzi had yet discovered, and that allowed a modicum of space for Meghan and Harry to begin the long, painful road to healing.

5

August and Everything After

Wildfire season roared through the area in August, with one nearby fire sparked by lightning strikes not far from Montecito. Harry and Meghan continued to work and recover privately. They would not be sharing their personal news with the world; at least not yet.

They were saddened, too, that August marked the end of their anonymity bubble. The media found out where they'd gone based on a deed filed by a trust connected to the duke and duchess. When the world learned of the Sussexes' precise location once again, their team put out a statement.

"They have settled into the quiet privacy of their community since their arrival and hope that this will be respected for their neighbors, as well as them for a family," a spokesperson for the couple pleaded.

By and large, their neighbors spoke out positively to welcome the family and showed no ill will toward the couple even though they'd bring an intrusive media wherever they went. A decades-long resident of Montecito told a newspaper that their moving in was "wonderful. It's a great idea for them if they seek anonymity and privacy."

Another long-time resident of the area, Judy Rossiter, told the *Daily Mail*, "I'm happy for them. Montecito is a beautiful place, ideal for raising a family. As for the 'impact' on our community, it's just another high-profile family for us and we will be respectful of their privacy."

They're bordered by billionaires, too. A stone's throw—or perhaps "a dog-toy's throw" is more apt considering the Sussexes' love of playing fetch with their pups—from their home is a huge spread owned by Peter and Stephanie Sperling. Peter made his fortune in part through online school University of Phoenix. Wealthy winemakers Igor and Cindy Sill are also nearby.

By September, though, reports filtered out that some locals weren't thrilled about the onslaught of paparazzi that have infiltrated Montecito and are "on the hunt for the shot" of the Sussexes, per TMZ. An area known for peace and quiet was plagued by the din of helicopters reportedly flying over Harry and Meghan's neighborhood several times a day and the entire area, including town, was infested with paparazzi. A more unofficial onslaught came to town too: your average royal watcher. Everyday citizens couldn't help themselves, and visited Santa Barbra and Montecito hoping for a glimpse of the resident royals.

Locals were "super annoyed" and were itching for the paparazzi to "give it a rest," according to TMZ. But just like that summer, neighbors didn't blame Meghan and Harry. Contrary to the tone of that report that they bore no ill will toward the couple. Rather than victim-blaming, they are as disgusted as the Sussexes are by the intrusive overkill brought on by the price tag on images of their heads and those of their child. The consensus by locals, at least early on, was to close ranks and help protect Meghan, Harry and Archie.

Unfortunately, no one knew just how much protecting the growing family would need.

It was a hot, dry summer's night. Meghan and Harry were fast asleep in the cozy master suite they'd decorated with relaxing creams and light patterns with pops of color in throw pillows; they'd laid the hardwood floors with a cozy carpet making for warm feet as they step out of bed every morning. It was a Zen retreat where the couple would recharge, reconnect, and snuggle with Archie on lazy Sunday mornings. But this night that haven couldn't buffer them from the realities of the harsh world outside.

Meghan bolted upright in bed. Harry still slept. She must have heard something; she *must* have. She arose, padded over to the window, and pulled the curtain aside.

Her security detail was downstairs and lights were moving about the property. "And so it begins," their security chief said tightly through clenched jaw.

And so it did. That's why the couple was so concerned about their royal protection being whipped away.

Meghan and Harry were generally shielded from such alarms; that's what security was there for. But she was always braced. With a baby in the house and open space all around them, racist threats, conspiracy theorists and violent people full of hate looking for a target, Meghan was always on the alert. There would be three more known security incidents that month alone, breaches that set them both on edge and reminded Harry why they were doing those big Netflix and Spotify deals in the first place. It wasn't because he needed a bigger mansion. It was because he needed a safer one. Though nothing bad happened that night, the security threats would continue. Police were called about their property nine times in nine months— that we know of. The British PA news agency obtained the records, which show police were called four times in July alone, which is noteworthy in that their address still hadn't hit the headlines yet.

The logs show a "phone request," plus several "alarm activations" which all came in the wee hours, and one August request is listed as "Misc Priority Incdnt."

Through all the upheaval, they kept working. Meghan invited feminist icon Gloria Steinem to her home for a chat about women's rights and voting rights that August, and Harry conducted a key Zoom call for the Invictus Games, his beloved international sporting events for wounded, injured and sick servicemen and women. No one outside their circle truly understood how they were continuing to be rattled by security threats.

Things were looking up on the September day when they signed their huge deal with Netflix. Said to be in the $100 million range, the contract lays out terms for the Sussexes' production company to create content over several years.

"Our focus will be on creating content that informs but also gives hope," the couple said in a statement. "As new parents, making inspirational family programming is also important to us." They added that Netflix's "unprecedented reach will help us share impactful content that unlocks action."

Both Harry and Meghan felt a wave of relief. For starters, they'd be able to pay back for renovations made to Frogmore Cottage, the home in Windsor which they ordered redecorated at a cost of millions to UK taxpayers—and now they'd be out of the line of fire after returning every single penny. But even more important than that, they could now afford protection for years to come.

Upon signing on the dotted line that September, Prince Harry grinned from ear to ear—he was filled with a sense of pride he hadn't been prepared for.

He'd *done* it; he'd found a way to keep his family safe after his sense of safety had been ripped away with little notice. As Harry would later say of the big content deals he and Meghan were making, "…my family literally cut me off financially, and I had to afford security for us." He added, "From my perspective, all I needed was enough money to be able to pay for security to keep my family safe."

Good show, Harry, old boy. *Good show.*

October in Santa Barbara was a beautiful time for the Sussexes. High season for tourists had passed, the air was clean and crisp, the wildfires were tamed, and they were well on their way to financial freedom. Though COVID-19 was still a huge threat around the world, people were learning how to navigate it by then, vaccines weren't far off, and there were some safer activities people felt comfortable joining in on. It was time to celebrate.

The couple ventured out on a cool, crisp evening for a much-needed date night. Meghan was physically healthy and well on her way to recovering emotionally from the shock and agony of her miscarriage, and autumn in Santa Barbara was still warm enough to eat comfortably outside. The couple, settled in and ready to explore their new community now that the first burst of press intrusion had calmed down somewhat, made plans for a double date with friends they could trust. Indeed, they expected to see a lot more of this particular couple now they were all in the same country.

Harry instructed their protection team to get on the case—this time with more advanced notice to avoid the similar scenario when they ran into a roadblock in the Vancouver restaurant—so the couple could enjoy a double date with music producer David Foster and his newly pregnant wife Katharine McPhee. Meghan and Katharine were friendly but not close back in the day, but had reconnected when she was in a musical production of *Waitress* in London's West End.

This was a big deal. Meghan and Harry's nights out had been severely limited since moving to the area. The miscarriage and its life-changing effects on the couple, the pandemic, and the extreme paparazzi intrusion had made for a lack of desire to plan and risk public socializing for the attention it was sure to draw. But that cool autumn

53

night they had old friends to meet, a comfortable safe space where they could be themselves and share their real lives and selves without fear of judgment or leaking to the media, and a reason to celebrate. Just that weekend it had been confirmed McPhee was expecting her first child (David's sixth).

With Archie tucked soundly in bed, Meghan stood barefoot on the soft carpeting inside her walk-in closet and selected an ensemble perfect for a mild fall night with a pre-winter chill to it, one that embodied Santa Barbara cool: cropped leather pants, a camel sweater and chic orange mules. Eventually, outside the restaurant, she would complete the look with a jaunty trench coat laid across her shoulders. Harry was equally, effortlessly not-try-too-hard stylish in basic dark trousers and a white shirt.

Meghan always took Harry's breath away, and as they stood waiting for the driver to bring the SUV around, he wrapped an arm around her and pulled her close. Their driver made the short trip to Lucky's Steakhouse in Montecito, an upscale local institution where a porterhouse steak will run you $125.

David and Katharine had already arrived, wearing masks in keeping with COVID-19 protocols, as did Meghan and Harry when they stepped out of the car a short time later. They were led out to the patio—and Meghan broke into a wide grin when she saw her old friend. They all embraced, removed their masks, and spent a full three hours catching up and talking about life and the pandemic and their children, and they all left at 10:30 p.m., firmer friends than ever.

6

For Better or Worse

The holidays were barreling toward them at warp speed. With the pandemic, Meghan couldn't do much of her beloved entertaining but they saw family and trusted friends, and planned for Thanksgiving with Doria and their first Christmas as an independent family in a home they both chose and loved.

As 2020 hurtled toward its finish, Meghan realized she was ready to share her deeply personal miscarriage with the world in the hope it would help even one person who'd been suffering in silence. The duchess sat down and penned a wide-ranging piece for the New York *Times*, covering the challenges of 2020 as a whole, including the pandemic and the killings of George Floyd and Breonna Taylor. But first, she revealed what happened to her in July. The months in between lent perspective so that Meghan was able to frame the event as a wider conversation.

"In the pain of our loss, my husband and I discovered that in a room of 100 women, 10 to 20 of them will have suffered from miscarriage," she wrote. "Yet despite the staggering commonality of this pain, the conversation remains taboo, riddled with (unwarranted) shame, and perpetuating a cycle of solitary mourning. Some have bravely shared their stories; they have opened the door, knowing that when one person speaks truth, it gives license for all of us to do the same."

"This year has brought so many of us to our breaking points," she suggested. "So, this Thanksgiving, 'let us commit to asking others, 'Are you OK?'"

From a woman who opened herself up in such a raw and revealing way, it was encouraging to see the duke and duchess overwhelmed with support and condolences and people asking online if they are OK. *That* was nice. What *wasn't* nice was the (not unexpected) barrage of abuse that flowed after it like a river of mud and slime, fast and grimy and determined to bring down everything in its path. Online commentary slammed Meghan for sharing too much, and tore her to shreds for daring to ask for privacy over the years for her and her family—and then coming out with something so personal.

The duchess said nothing then.

But she had some things to say, and she said them in the big interview with Oprah.

The Sussexes are involved in the same tug-of-war that celebrities have engaged in for decades: what do they "owe" the public whose attention they actively court? Without our attention on them, there are no multi-million-dollar Netflix or Spotify deals. The road to attracting the precise "right" attention is strewn with potholes. One thing is certain: You court the international attention, you're going to get more than you bargained for.

In which case, you can fight back.

Meghan instructed her lawyers to launch a privacy claim against Associated Newspapers Limited, which publishes *The Mail on Sunday* and *MailOnline,* in 2019. The suit had first been revealed as they completed a royal tour in southern Africa in September 2019, at which point the world heard Meghan was suing the *Mail on Sunday* for publishing a private letter she sent to her father, Thomas Markle, after the royal wedding in 2018.

"We have initiated legal proceedings against the *Mail on Sunday,* and its parent company Associated Newspapers, over the intrusive and unlawful publication of a private letter written by the Duchess of Sussex, which is part of a campaign by this media group to publish false and deliberately derogatory stories about her, as well as her husband," a legal spokesperson for the couple said in a statement when the suit was filed. "Given the refusal of Associated Newspapers to resolve this issue satisfactorily, we have issued proceedings to redress this breach of privacy, infringement of copyright, and the aforementioned media agenda."

Later in the week it was confirmed by Buckingham Palace that Harry had filed a lawsuit of his own over an alleged phone and voicemail hacking in the early 2000s. Harry released a statement of his own: "The contents of a private letter were published unlawfully in an intentionally destructive manner to manipulate you, the reader, and further the divisive agenda of the media group in question," Harry said. "In addition to their unlawful publication of this private document, they purposely misled you by strategically omitting select paragraphs, specific sentences, and even singular words to mask the lies they had perpetuated for over a year."

On February 11, 2021, Meghan won her lawsuit (the newspaper announced it planned to appeal). In his ruling, the judge said that Meghan had a "reasonable expectation that the contents of the letter would remain private" and that therefore the actions of the *Mail and Sunday* and the *MailOnline* were "unlawful."

Meghan quickly put out a statement:

"After two long years of pursuing litigation, I am grateful to the courts for holding Associated Newspapers and *The Mail on Sunday* to account for their illegal and dehumanizing practices," the statement read. "These tactics (and those of their sister publications *MailOnline* and the *Daily Mail*) are not new; in fact, they've been going on for far too long without consequence. For these outlets, it's a game. For me and so many others, it's real life, real relationships, and very real sadness. The damage they have done and continue to do runs deep.

"The world needs reliable, fact-checked, high-quality news. What *The Mail on Sunday* and its partner publications do is the opposite," her statement continued. "We all lose when misinformation sells more than truth, when moral exploitation sells more than decency, and when companies create their business model to profit from people's pain.

But for today, with this comprehensive win on both privacy and copyright, we have all won. We now know, and hope it creates legal precedent, that you cannot take somebody's privacy and exploit it in a privacy case, as the defendant has blatantly done over the past two years."

That poignant victory was in February 2021.

In March of 2021, Meghan and Harry were ready to reclaim their own story and speak their own truths over the reams of anonymous leaks that had targeted them for years. In her interview with Oprah, Meghan addressed the constant snickering over her right to privacy.

"I've never talked about privacy," she said. "They've created a false narrative. I've *never* talked about privacy."

The couple is asserting their basic right to privacy in sharing the "parts of their lives" they were "comfortable" with giving the public access to—just like the rest of us.

"'There's no one who's on Instagram or social media that would say, 'Because I shared this one picture, that entitles you to have my entire camera roll. Go ahead and look through it.' No one would want that. So it's about boundaries. And it's about respect."

Some hit back that if you are going to put yourself and your children out there for personal gain, you must take what comes. You can't eat your cake and have it, too, critics say. The man at the office in her example showing one photo of his child to a co-worker is not making money off that share, nor is he using it to build his brand. Of course, that doesn't matter. Meghan is a human being with all the rights and power that affords. She gets to set *her* boundaries. You don't have to like it. But she's asserted her agency and she's not going to cower to anyone's attempt to take it away from her, and you *do* have to deal with it.

Back to November 2020, a time when *anyone* could pinpoint the Sussexes' exact location, the nerve-jangling intruder alarms weren't abating and at least one came that month. Still, they thrived. Harry reveled in heading to the beach with Archie and the dogs even into the winter months, something he'd rarely do back home this time of year (thought it didn't stop the royals from seaside cold-weather walks in their various homes).

Work-wise, Harry and Meghan were still working on projects and deals, and that December they launched a website for Archewell, which also included information about its nonprofit branch and their Spotify podcast along with the Sussexes' production company. On a personal level, they made a big deal of creating their first American Christmas card and involved little Archie in all the decorations and plans as appropriate.

Grandma Doria brought her camera down to the children's cottage not long before Christmas. Two potted, ornamented trees with red bows—Archie chose the decorations. Two dogs. Lots of smiles. Doria clicked away until she captured the ideal moment as the family was joyfully playing around Archie's playhouse, and the image was animated and turned into a family Christmas card. When the holidays were over, the trees would be replanted.

The couple made sure the very personal card brought something good to the world. They allowed one of Meghan's patronages, the UK-based Mayhew animal rescue, to release it, thus bringing a tsunami of positive publicity to an amazing cause.

The world could see the smiles and the wagging dog and the happy baby. But they couldn't see through those smiles to the new level of joy—tempered by *some* trepidation—Harry and Meghan were carrying privately. For Meghan was pregnant again and feeling great. They were nowhere near ready to share the news, but they were over the moon to be expecting again.

And then things got very, very dark.

Any holiday cheer mustered up in the dark pandemic year of 2020 was smashed to smithereens when, at four in the afternoon on Christmas Eve, presents under the tree, grandma Doria in the house, and Santa on his way, an intruder burst onto their property. Deputies were immediately called, and Santa Barbara's finest raced to the house. Meghan, Harry, Doria, Archie and their staff hunkered down inside as they waited for police to arrive.

When they did, officers quickly removed the man and gave him a warning. Then they let him go.

But the trespasser, who turned out to be Ohio resident Nickolas Brooks, 37, wasn't done with the Sussexes—though they didn't know that. Harry, Meghan and the family took a breath and went back to celebrating, talking to Archie about the meaning of Christmas, and FaceTiming friends and family who they couldn't be with that holiday.

They rose early on Christmas Day to find Santa's presents under the tree and the cookies and carrots Archie had left for Santa and the reindeer were gone. It was a lovely, lively and private affair. The family spent Boxing Day—the Brits' way of making the day after Christmas, Dec. 26, a holiday, one the U.S. should get too, frankly—much the same way, minus Santa. Again, all was well.

That is, until 2:45 p.m. That was when Nikolas Brooks came back. He was, this time, arrested and charged with one count of misdemeanor trespassing. This call to police was categorized as "Property Crimes."

What was he after? Why was he harassing the Sussex family, and why did he think he had the right to intrude on their peaceful home?

The world learned the story from the U.K. tabloid *The Sun*. Brooks chattered away, explaining that he might have been "high" at the time, and revealing to The Sun that he once took part in an attack that left a man with a broken bone in his face.

"I don't know why I went to their place, that's kind of where I ended up," Brooks said. "I drove across the country—I know it's crazy. I've been told to stay away and that I'm never allowed back there but I don't have to appear in court. I was in jail for a night and they told me to stay away in future."

7

New year, new changes

Winter turned to spring and the world began to wake up as the vaccination process crept slowly around the globe. Meghan was, as she had been with Archie, sometimes exhausted from her pregnancy. Unlike her sister-in-law Kate, who was hospitalized for hyperemesis gravidarum (characterized by extreme "morning sickness" including vomiting) during her pregnancy with George, Meghan didn't battle much nausea. Although her appetite, sources suggest, was affected in unsurprising ways, sometimes reduced and sometimes a bit fiercer than normal, sometimes quirky (i.e the old pickles-and-ice-cream type of cravings people talk about during pregnancy).

Meghan continued to center herself with yoga, something she could always return to when she needed to reset and recharge.

But it was the fatigue that was tough. When she and Harry visited Bondi Beach on an Australia trip when she was expecting Archie, Meghan admitted to onlookers that she'd had a particularly early start, having woken up at 4:30

am that morning. One royal fan who was also pregnant at the time talked to the duchess about the experience, and after they'd met, the woman revealed to press that "Meghan told me that pregnancy was like having jet lag. She said she was up at 4:30…doing yoga in her room as she couldn't sleep. It's a bit of a double whammy for her, she said, as she has both the baby and jet lag to contend with."

On that same trip, Meghan confessed to young mother Emily Carroll that "she's feeling pretty good so far, which is great. She said they're doing 76 engagements in 16 days, with maybe one rest in the middle. She's made for this royal business, isn't she?" Carroll also made a point of telling the media that Harry and Meghan are "both great with kids."

Meghan kept that smile on no matter how exhausted she was. "I'm running on adrenaline," she admitted.

The couple had agreed with the Queen that they were in a sort of one-year trial period of "stepping away" from senior royal duties. In February 2021, the door that had been left open for Harry and Meghan's possible return was closed.

"Following conversations with The Duke, The Queen has written confirming that in stepping away from the work of The Royal Family it is not possible to continue with the responsibilities and duties that come with a life of public service," the palace announced.

The Sussex response was swift and declarative and became a social media siren call of sorts among the couple's fans:

"We can all live a life of service. Service is universal," a Sussex spokesperson said.

Around the same time, the couple reached a point where they felt safe enough to share their happy news that they were expecting again. While no due date was provided, many educated guesses suggested she was likely due in summer.

Settled in, healthy, and knowing a daughter was on the way to complete their family in the most enviably perfect way, they commissioned Meghan's longtime friend Misan Harriman to capture their announcement in a safely distanced manner: On a tablet from across a continent and an ocean.

In the photo, the smiling parents are posing yet relaxed under a gorgeous tree. With Harry sitting in the grass, shoes off, Meghan lays back with her head on his lap.

When Oprah Winfrey and CBS announced in February 2021 that the Duke and Duchess of Sussex would be doing a sit-down with the Queen of Daytime, the heads of royal watchers the world over pretty much exploded.

It was teed up by CBS so well that it was quickly seen as the most anticipated primetime television interview in years, if not decades, as buzz built up to a crescendo of expectation. Which was fun for us, but apparently terrifying for a certain British family with several palaces and castles in their portfolio.

Indeed, the report of a no-holds-barred interview, the content of which remained a complete mystery at that point, made some very important people back in London nervous. It appeared the various palaces were going on the offensive, though the negative commentary pouring out of Britain was mostly anonymous and/or vaguely sourced.

It got so bad that the media, and/or the various palaces, were no longer happy with vague or weak storylines put out to slam the Oprah interview before it happened. The British royals went nuclear in an apparent attempt to discredit Meghan and Harry before anyone even knew what they would say. This move made a lot of us wonder: If no one knew what the Sussexes were going to say, why the need to go on the offensive? Could there be secrets the Palaces (Buckingham, Kensington, Clarence House, and what have you) didn't want Meghan and Harry revealing, and if so, didn't that mean that by definition the secrets could be expected to be *true*?

But as Meghan herself would shrug and say in an early promo for the interview, "I don't know how they could expect that after all of this time, we would still just be silent if there is an active role that 'the firm' is playing in perpetuating falsehoods about us. If that comes with risk of losing things…I mean, there's a lot that's been lost already."

The Firm entered freak-out mode, as much as stone-faced posh Brits can get into freak-out mode. Out blasted an explosive story in the UK's broadsheet the *Times*. In it, the reporter wrote that a former royal aide to Meghan and still working with the Cambridges—royal press secretary Jason Knauf, a Texas native—filed a complaint with the palace in October 2018, accusing her of bullying her staff, reducing some junior aides to tears, and driving two personal assistants out of the royal household.

"I am very concerned that the Duchess was able to bully two PAs out of the household in the past year," Knauf wrote to Prince William's private secretary Simon Case, after first raising concerns with Samantha Carruthers, the head of HR, the *Times* reported.

"The Duchess seems intent on always having someone in her sights," he continued. "She is bullying Y (name removed) and seeking to undermine her confidence...I remain concerned that nothing will be done."

Prince Harry allegedly met with Knauf and begged him not to pursue the complaints—Prince Harry has denied this.

Buckingham Palace then brought the 2018 alleged complaints into the present, and shortly before the Oprah interview, they announced a probe into the allegations. In its statement on the bullying claims, Buckingham Palace said, "The Royal Household has had a Dignity at Work policy in place for a number of years and does not, and will not, tolerate bullying or harassment in the workplace."

This was all going on while Prince Philip was laid up in the hospital at age 99 with heart problems. No one outside the UK *Times* could prove who was leaking it, but we knew who could stop it from leaking, the New York *Times* reported. "This tap could be turned off," Peter Hunt, a former royal correspondent for the BBC, said. "The Buckingham Palace bit of it could be turned off in a nanosecond."

The announcement was, in fact, an ill-advised act of desperation that any competent public relations advisor could see would end badly. Buckingham Palace insisted it was "very concerned" about the allegations, would look into them and invited former staff members of the couple to take part in the investigation "to see if lessons can be learned."

The idea the family's HR department would investigate such a high-profile target as Meghan received the side-eye from some corners. After all, if you start digging, you might turn up embarrassing scraps that prompt others within The Firm to feel safe making their own complaints.

"They have opened an unbelievable can of worms," royal observer Hunt told the New York *Times*. "Are they really going to find her guilty of bullying? Will it be in the form of a #MeToo investigation? It really feels like the anarchists have taken over the institution."

If Britain was in a bitter uproar, Americans were waiting eagerly with anticipation and popcorn—and they were defending their own. Said Oprah herself about their desire to speak out: "I think they agreed to do it, wanted to do it, were ready to do it because when you have been lied about for a series of years—I think anybody can understand this—if in your own office or in your own family, somebody is saying things about you that are not true and how hurtful that is, or if you're online and you read the comments from something that somebody has said about you and you continue to see those comments, how hurtful that is. So imagine that for over a period of months and years and you *know* that it isn't true."

Meghan tried not to read or watch news reports about the reaction to her and Harry's forthcoming interview. But word got to her about these stinging bullying allegations. With something so huge, so hurtful, and so damaging, it was inevitable she'd be informed of the news that she was being accused of bullying—as she should.

She had a right to respond, and her team did, quickly and plainly with a statement to the world from their spokesperson: "The Duchess is saddened by this latest attack on her character, particularly as someone who has been the target of bullying herself and is deeply committed to supporting those who have experienced pain and trauma."

Meghan had some sort of say, but it didn't seem to do much at the time. She was not OK.

It was a cool night in Montecito when she simply couldn't pretend anymore. Spring was right around the corner—and so was the March 7 airdate for Meghan and Harry's big Oprah interview. The pair were tucked cozily in their king-sized bed in their mansion. All would have appeared well to an onlooker on that quiet night, but Meghan was far from a peaceful slumber. She and Harry had taken back their lives and chosen the most effective and trustworthy outlet to tell their own story—and Meghan found peace and power in that. This night, though, she was ill-at-ease and felt a nagging dread. Nothing was ever straightforward, it seemed. Nothing they did, no matter how well-meaning, seemed to please their detractors.

Meghan lay awake and felt a tsunami of anxiety engulf her. She turned over, planted her face in her pillow, and bawled. She fought to not wake her husband, but he sensed something was wrong or heard her muffled sobs and woke anyway. It was the middle of the night and he was alarmed.

He held her, and when she caught her breath she told him what was the matter. Meghan had gone through a pandemic, a move, a barrage of hurtful media attacks, a miscarriage, security scares, and now she was heavily pregnant and being accused of the one thing she strove never to be a part of. She wasn't out to hurt people.

She was powerless against this particular force that was, as Harry would say, the "combined effort of the firm and the media to smear her."

He would later recount the emotional interaction in the docuseries *The Me You Can't See* on AppleTV+ which he co-created with Oprah, adding that Meghan didn't want "to wake me up, because I'm already carrying too much. That's heartbreaking. I held her, we talked, she cried, and she cried, and she cried."

It turned out the Palace was right to be worried about this epic, sprawling, revelatory and honest two-hour interview that went 'round the world. Meghan and Harry covered everything.

Everything.

They took time to clarify the ongoing narrative that they'd flown off in an irresponsible huff from their duties in the UK.

"It's been so spun in the wrong direction as though we quit, we walked away," Meghan said. "We never left the family. We said specifically, 'We're stepping back from senior roles to be just like several [other royals]'.... We weren't reinventing the wheel here. We were saying, 'Okay, if this isn't working for everyone. We're in a lot of pain. You can't provide us with the help that we need. We can just take a step back. We can do it in a Commonwealth country.'"

Prince Harry said he needed a break "from this constant barrage" of scrutiny. "My biggest concern was history repeating itself," he said, referring to his mother Princess Diana's death during a car chase by paparazzi. "And what I was seeing was history repeating itself, but far more dangerous because you add race and social media in." He continued, "To receive no help at all and to be told continuously, 'This is how it is. This is just how it is. We've all been through it,'" was frustrating.

Meghan stressed to her fans that she hopes the message people take from the interview is "know there's another side, to know that life is worth living."

There was, of course, so much more shared that day, and the fallout from their honesty was both inspiring—people dealing with mental health issues, BIPOC who were sick of being gaslit and told they don't face racism in their everyday lives, women who were sick of having their voices ignored all thanked the couple—and horrendous.

Meghan and Harry's revelations broadcast across the globe were explosive, but the world within their walls was calm. On the night the interview aired, Meghan kept to her regular routine, reading to Archie—a favorite at the time was *Duck! Rabbit!*—and tucking him in. As he began to settle, she sat with him alone in the quiet as millions of people watched her project her truth to Oprah Winfrey's empathetic and analytical ear. Rather than interrupt bedtime by turning on the TV or trawling social media, Meghan texted Oprah with the most casual of inquiries: *Putting Archie to bed. No idea what's happening with the east coast feed. How's it going?*

Oprah wrote back right away: *I don't either. From what I can tell, it's going well, I know it's airing.*

How it was going was a mixed bag of extreme hot-takes and absolute jaw-dropping disbelief, fury and online abuse directed at the couple. People were angry for different reasons. Americans largely responded with horror that the duchess, one of their own, felt trapped and like she didn't want to live anymore, was subjected to racist abuse, and had her own son's skin color brought up at all, let alone questioned in a vile manner by his own blood relatives.

Harry's home country roared up, aghast, catastrophizing, *tsk*ing or accusing. Picking apart Meghan's words story became a refreshed pastime of the British media.

Just as quickly, mid-interview in fact, defenders rose up and built a protective wall of support. They believed Meghan. They cried for her. People who had survived or had considered attempting suicide felt her pain and reached out and spoke up. If nothing else, this was something to be taken seriously. Palace gates and family jewels do not a perfect life make. A royal title is not a cure for depression. Sometimes, a royal title is a catalyst for it.

One anecdote Meghan shared that got people riled up was about a private wedding they had before the "spectacle" of the royal affair everyone else saw. "We called the Archbishop, and we just said, 'Look, this thing, this spectacle is for the world, but we want our union between us'. So, like, the vows that we have framed in our room are just the two of us in our backyard with the Archbishop of Canterbury," Meghan said. That shocked a lot of people— and also upset them for some unknown reason. A British tabloid went for their own "aha!" moment by revealing the legal marriage certificate was given on May 19, the day of the televised ceremony (congratulations for making it down the clerk's office, by the way!), calling Meghan a liar for saying otherwise.

By March 23, Meghan and Harry felt compelled to release a statement addressing the relentless questioning of the story about marrying three days before their public marriage. A spokesperson told *The Daily Beast* that yes, the earlier affair wasn't a legal marriage but that "the couple exchanged personal vows a few days before their official/legal wedding on May 19."

Piers Morgan, who has written a disturbing amount of copy and social media posts about the Duchess over the past few years, who almost obsessively discusses the fact he had one drink with her at a pub once and could never get her attention again, possibly signaling a frightening fixation with the former Meghan Markle, this time Tweeted a link to a story headlined "Harry and Meghan's claim that they wed in secret is blown apart by their own marriage certificate" and wrote, "Do we still have to believe her?"

The response from the couple's defenders was swift. Once again they posited it was not that Meghan had offered an untruth, but that she shared *her* truth. They pointed out it wasn't that it mattered not if she was "caught" in something, but that the is the only one whose words are parsed into oblivion and every claim researched like it was life-or-death—unlike any other royal.

One England-based Twitter response to Morgan's continued investment in Meghan Markle read, "It was clearly a sweet private exchange of vows that they cherish and consider their day. Genuine question why do you feel so triggered by her? Consider is it connecting you back to the time you were rejected before?"

The topic of the wedding was one more chance to flame the couple over just so much fluff. The more sinister revelations, the barbs no one knew Meghan was fending off while she was smiling and working hard at all those royal engagements and patronages, was about as-yet-unborn Archie's skin tone. Readers might have the same reaction Oprah did to such vile thinking, which was to almost spontaneously combust with horror.

"In those months when I was pregnant…[there were] concerns and conversations about how dark his skin might be when he was born," Meghan said, refusing to say who it was. "I think that would be very damaging to them."

Later in the interview, Oprah pushed Harry for details. "That conversation, I'm never going to share," he replied. "But the timing was awkward; I was a bit shocked." He added it "was right at the beginning, when [Meghan] wasn't going to get security, when members of my family were suggesting that she carries on acting because there's not enough money to pay for her."

Also that night, Kate was brought into the discourse. The old story of Kate being pushed to tears during a confrontation before Meghan's wedding was turned on its head: Meghan says it was she, in fact, who burst into tears due to Kate being hard on her. The fact that no one from The Firm corrected the story and they wouldn't let Meghan correct the story was part of the reason they left England.

But it was the race row dominated the discourse more than any of the rest. William was reportedly "raging" about it, and couldn't help but respond when questions were shouted at him during an engagement soon after the interview: "We are very much not a racist family," he said, giving them what they wanted, jaw clenched, defensive posture, no hint of self-reflection or insight.

"Who said it?" began trending online immediately, and the question would pop up for months to come. It was quickly deduced by those in the know that it was likely *not* Prince Philip, in part because, had it been Phillip who said it, there would be very little shock or surprise about that considering his past racist behavior. No, it had to be a person who wouldn't be seen saying anything so obvious in a public setting, royal sleuths decided. Still, some did bat around Philip's name, along with Charles's and William's. Most likely to say that to Harry, in our humble opinion (again, the royal family has denied saying racist things), could be Charles—*if* it was said.

In a thinking-person's take, *The New Yorker* ran a story asking, "Who did this unnamed member of the family think would mind if Archie had dark skin? Perhaps more important, has this royal ever really recognized the many Britons who might feel more connected to the family if Archie didn't look like countless other descendants of Queen Victoria? (A reminder of the strangeness of the institution: Elizabeth and Philip are both Victoria's great-great-grandchildren.)"

Amy Davidson Sorkin's piece also suggested Meghan had simply reminded us what we already knew to be true. It certainly seemed the gloss was suddenly-but-not-so-suddenly peeling away, that in modern times it wasn't worth the glamour and historical drama for the damage it did to individuals. Rather than an amusing bunch of harmless, attractive and loveable rogues, was the British royal family actually an anachronistic toxin?

"Instead, the monarchy is the attenuated remnant of an institution that was, in centuries past, despotic and repugnant to democracy, and shaped and misshaped by the luck of inheritance," Sorkin wrote. "Because the political power that was once attached to kings and queens is (mostly) gone, it is easy to get used to the idea that the persistence of the monarchy is harmless, and maybe even useful. Power, after all, makes the difference between terror and petty cruelty."

She suggests British subjects could use the interview as a chance to step back and think for themselves about what use they actually are and, "For Americans, it raises another question: why did we ever find all of this so amusing. It seemed fun, for one thing, and it was pretty."

Indeed, through all of the panic and drama, the young ones, particularly those outside the UK, began to make it clear the anachronistic ways were falling out of fashion.

Generation Z is unimpressed with the monarchy. They're calling it like they see it. One American TikTok star put up a background of Meghan's face and leveled a cool gaze at the camera: "What crusty old man is looking at *her* [and is] worried about the gene pool in the family?"

Then the TikToker next put up the British royal family tree and pointed out there aren't, um, so many branches, actually. "Have we looked at the family tree and how it is circular and not a tree? Not only is queen Elizabeth and her husband Prince Philip cousins, but both parents on both sides are *alllll* related." In conclusion, they said, it seems like the royal family is saying, "We don't care about incest…and not pedophilia or sex trafficking."

With the monarchy appearing increasingly out of touch and losing its once-global glow of glamour and dignity, with Charles and Williams' perceived preference of status quo over inclusion, of sweeping under the carpet instead of evolving, it was beginning to seem like Meghan and Harry's new independent way of making a living—and a life—could very well one day be less a novelty and more the norm.

All of that said, you almost wouldn't know it, but during the Oprah interview there was some levity and sweetness, too. Along with revealing they were having a girl, which thrilled Oprah and every fan who watched the program, they also showed off some of their home. The relatively new parents had created another teachable bonding activity to do with Archie. They could visit the chickens, and later would be able to collect freshly laid eggs. Sources say it came to be when Meghan watched Archie toddle about, examine the coop under construction, and then it came to her.

She giggled with joy when she tried out the line on Harry and their son: "What about if we called this 'Archie's Chick Inn?'" The idea was a hit, and the public would get a close look at the sign they commissioned to christen the coop during outtakes from the Oprah interview.

"Hi, girls!" Meghan said as she opened the door to the coop to introduce them to Oprah. Of course, the media titan immediately took note of the sign: "Archie's Chick Inn — established 2021."

"I just love rescuing," Meghan told her.

The Sussex family created a comfortable place for the factory farm rescues, and the duchess immediately began calling them her "girls." (Understandably, when the world heard Meghan talk so fondly of her new pets, even some of her staunchest allies on social media winced: "Let's hope she's not roasting chickens anymore," wrote one, in a clear reference to her engagement interview where she and Harry claimed to have eaten chicken on the night he proposed).

8

The aftermath

When it was all over, the world awoke the next morning and waited with bated breath for Buckingham Palace to respond. And they waited. And they waited. Royal reporters champed at the bit to be able to report something, anything, new about palace reaction. All they could do was post about their own frustration. *Express* royal reporter Richard Palmer Tweeted, "Plenty to write and not much time to tweet today. Crisis meetings continue in the Royal Household. Every single person authorised to speak to the media has their phone switched off, as far as I can tell. And it's not just me they aren't taking calls from."

It was two interminable days before official word came out from The Firm.

In a statement, Buckingham Palace said on behalf of the Queen, "The whole family is saddened to learn the full extent of how challenging the last few years have been for Meghan and Harry. The issues raised, particularly that of race, are concerning. While some recollections may vary, they are taken very seriously and will be addressed by the family privately. Harry, Meghan, and Archie will always be much loved family members."

When asked about it when he was seen out and about, Prince Charles "chuckled" and walked away.

The post-interview frenzy around the pair continued at warp speed. Harry had said flatly that the British tabloids had created a "toxic environment" of fear and control. That was hard to argue with when headlines like "Harry's girl is (almost) straight outta Compton" and "Harry to marry into gangster royalty?" rolling casually off the presses.

In the interview, Meghan summarized the couple's view of much of the British media: "From the beginning of our relationship, they were so attacking and incited so much racism."

But powerful voices in the UK media weren't ready to hear those truths. Too many went on the defensive instead of listening, learning and stepping outside of their own experiences. Ian Murray, executive director of media industry group the Society of Editors, felt the need to respond to the Sussexes' brave revelations with a statement lacking any modicum of insight.

Murray, who is white, said the claims were "not acceptable" and made without "supporting evidence." He felt the need to blast out the idea that the UK media "has a proud record of calling out racism." In a piece headlined "UK media not bigoted" he said the tone of tabloid coverage was simply driven by "holding a spotlight up to those in positions of power, celebrity or influence."

Ah, but not everyone was going to let that slide. A full 168 Britain-based journalists, writers and broadcasters of color joined together for their own statement to slam Murray's ludicrous response.

"The blanket refusal to accept there is any bigotry in the British press is laughable, does a disservice to journalists of colour, and shows an institution and an industry in denial," read the open letter.

Ultimately, the consensus out of the UK was simple and cohesive: Harry and Meghan should never have shared their stories. A quiet royal is a good royal.

Obviously, the discussion couldn't be complete without Prince Albert of Monaco chiming in. He wasn't happy, *no sirree*. Albert peppered his distaste with some quasi-supportive words, but it wasn't enough to mask the bitter taste his comments left. He "can understand the pressure that they were under," but said that "these types of conversations should be held within the intimate quarters of the family" and "it doesn't really have to be laid out in the public sphere like that."

"It did bother me a little bit," he said of the Oprah chat. "I can understand where they're coming from in a certain way, but I think it wasn't the appropriate forum to be able to have these kinds of discussions."

The message came through loud and clear: be quiet. A woman, an American, a biracial person. The comfort of those around her is more important than the mental health and justice for Meghan and Harry.

As Sussex Squad member calling herself Anne Boleyn pointed out on March 26, "I'm not surprised that Prince Albert, a man with [one] biracial [child] out of wedlock & exempt from having any titles, is criticizing Meghan & Harry. That's all I'm going to say....."

The British media wasted no time calling on Meghan's estranged family, who they have on speed-dial, to add fuel to the flames and squeeze any last drops of knowledge from the family well. It was drying up, to be sure; the duchess hadn't spoken to any of them in months, or even years, by that point.

The Sussexes went on with their lives, though they did chat with Gayle King of CBS This Morning and with Oprah, as well, during the fallout. The week after the show aired, King came out and revealed she'd been in touch with the couple over the previous weekend and things hadn't gone particularly well, especially with William and Charles.

"Harry has talked to his brother and he has talked to his father, too. The word I was given was those conversations were not productive," King said. "But they are glad that they have at least started a conversation."

While Harry and Meghan wanted an open dialogue, the palace was still intent on sweeping everything uncomfortable under the rug.

"I think what is still upsetting to them is that the palace keeps saying they want to work it out privately, but yet they believe these false stories are coming out that are very disparaging against Meghan still." And she went on to share that the royal family hadn't talked to Meghan directly.

King added, "all they wanted all along was for the royals to intervene and tell the press to stop with the unfair, inaccurate, false stories that definitely have a racial slant. And until you can acknowledge that, I think it's going to be hard to move forward. But they both want to move forward with this…At the end of the day, that is Harry's family."

King also discussed the bullying claims alleged by palace staff. "The bullying thing was raised in 2018, and now there's an ongoing investigation about bullying for Meghan Markle, when anyone who has worked with her will tell you exactly who she is—you know, she's really a very sweet, caring person," King said. "And, as I say, Meghan has documents to back up everything that she said on Oprah's interview. Everything."

As for what Meghan and Harry hope will happen in the future, King explained, "The family has to acknowledge that there are issues, and right now, no one is acknowledging, 'Houston, we have a problem here.' That's really all they want. They want a conversation."

For those who aren't Sussex "stans" but pay attention, to those who find the racism against the family abhorrent but aren't huge royal followers, there was a clear view that not every word out of both of their mouths would be perfect and not in dispute with the family in England. But rather than spending time trying to catch her in lies or misstatements or things not everyone wants to believe, Meghan's supporters—and supporters of girls and women of color by extension—tried to keep the focus on the racism and misogyny she's faced. Rather than pick her apart, they say, *listen* to her. Instead of questioning the veracity of her talk of suicide, empathize. Instead of investigating her claims at a time when it appears the royals have closed ranks on an alleged sex offender eighth in line for the throne.

Some also suggested the ongoing attacks on her were direct attempts to distract from the high-profile accused criminal in the family—Prince Andrew.

"The Palace's total failure to protect Meghan—by not defending her in the press, by not ensuring she and her child received adequate security, and by preventing her from checking in to a treatment center when she asked for help—stands in stark contrast to how it has consistently rallied around another member of the royal family: Prince Andrew, the Queen's second son and an accused sex offender," wrote Madeleine Aggeler in *New York* magazine's The Cut.

Andrew, considered to be a favorite of his mother Queen Elizabeth, has close ties to the late convicted pedophile Jeffrey Epstein. In one denial his camp put out, there was a statement that 'he doesn't sweat.' The internet promptly produced photos of Prince Andrew sweating profusely.

Virginia (Roberts) Giuffre told the BBC's Panorama in 2019 that when she was 17 years old she was trafficked by Epstein and forced to have sex with his friends, including Andrew, the Duke of York. Giuffre also accused the prince, who has repeatedly denied the allegations, of lying about their encounter and urged the British public to back her over Andrew.

"I'm calling BS on this, because that's what it is," she said. "He knows what happened. I know what happened, and there's only one of us telling the truth, and I know that's me," she told the BBC.

But Buckingham Palace denied her allegations in a statement to CNN.

"It is emphatically denied that The Duke of York had any form of sexual contact or relationship with Virginia Roberts. Any claim to the contrary is false and without foundation," they said.

In an interview with Sky, royal reporter Carolyn Durand pointed out, "Why hasn't he been urged to cooperate with U.S. authorities? Why were Prince Harry's military honors stripped but Prince Andrew's haven't been?"

9

To everything there is a season

Meghan has spoken often and eloquently about women's reduced opportunity in the workplace—and in life—especially for Black women and women of color. Wonderful women directors—there are so many, but so few are given opportunities. Women of color in entertainment—so many are qualified, too many are held back.

On Global Citizen's web page, a contributor posted an article lauding Meghan's outspoken support: "Markle's story reinforced the notion that **allyship cannot be effectively demonstrated with statements, platitudes, and promises alone, but that decisive action must be taken** in order to advance equity, inclusion, a sense of belonging, and safety for all."

And so, as Women's History Month 2021 wound down, the couple's charitable organization Archewell announcement of a key appointment under its umbrella made some supporters bristle. Ben Browning joined the nonprofit in a massive flagship position as the head of content overseeing Archewell Productions and Archewell

Audio. He is expected to work closely alongside Netflix and Spotify to help bring their respective creative partnerships with the video and audio streaming giants—including television shows, films, and podcasts—to fruition. He joined executive director James Holt as another white male in the two top Archewell positions.

"Taking nothing away from the skills of Mr. Browning, it feels like the Sussexes really missed a chance there to show they mean what they say when they talk about empowering women and BIPOC," said one well-connected observer. "Surely there were some women of color available and qualified for such a key appointment; and what progress it would've been."

Countered another source, "The Archewell team is diverse. We aren't privy to the plans and discussions going on within the organization and with the duke and duchess, so let's wait and see before we jump on this particular appointment."

Sussex supporters, even those who felt tense inside about the choice, kept relatively quiet on this one, at least in public. As frequent Sussex supporter Goldburn P. Maynard Jr. explained on Twitter later when talking about the squad's habit of hanging back from pointing out anything negative no matter how factually true, "I think we partly have an Obama problem where someone is criticized in such an over the top way that supporters don't want to bring up legitimate concerns because it adds to the negative voices and it's further used against them. Thus, why some people talk behind the scenes."

In any case, Archewell was up and running, ready to start putting out the quality content fans are expecting.

But there was more. Around the same time, a Silicon Valley company announced that Harry would be taking on the most California role a thirty-something guy could: a "Chief Impact Officer" for a tech startup. He'd be holding a real-life day job with BetterUp, which offers coaching and mental health services.

The company described Harry this way on its website: as a "humanitarian, military veteran, mental wellness advocate, and environmentalist." Harry was set to contribute to product strategy decisions and charitable contributions—perhaps most important of all, he'd be able to continue his and advocate publicly on topics related to mental health, the newspaper reported. Though they were asked, BetterUp did not reveal any hints about Harry's compensation package.

"What caught my attention about BetterUp was that the company's mission to unlock the potential in people everywhere necessitates innovation, impact, and integrity. Their team has been delivering on that work for years," said Harry.

Author and journalist Bolu Babalola captured the prince-goes-to-Silicon-Valley energy, Tweeting, "I love that Harry is working for a tech start up now LOL yes, tech bro is his destiny."

Some gently mocked the prince, like feminist website *Jezebel* with an amusing take on his new gig: "In his new, definitely real role Harry will be 'expected to have input into initiatives including product strategy decisions and charitable contributions, and advocate publicly on topics related to mental health.'

"These are real tasks for a real job. Despite having no experience at a start-up, no tech experience, and no background in any work related to mental health, the company is excited about their new 'officer of the corporation' and welcomes him with open arms into this 'meaningful and meaty' job."

By and large, though, the overriding reaction among those who respected the couple was to congratulate Harry for getting a "real" job while others in his own family were content to live off public and generational money.

Harry also said he had personally benefited from coaching provided by BetterUp. "I've personally found working with a BetterUp coach to be invaluable. I was matched with a truly awesome coach who has given me sound advice and a fresh perspective," the duke said in the blog post.

Everyone had an opinion on the move. UK talent agent Jonathan Shalit, whose bio says he's worked with stars from Elton John to former Spice Girl Mel B, posited that Harry felt a need to be on equal footing with his accomplished wife.

"For Harry to keep up with his wife, he's got to find his own name and identity and this is the start," Shalit told *The Telegraph* newspaper. Meghan, the agent pointed out, is "a hugely astute woman, very bright…" and "incredibly impressive."

All true. And so far, after taking that leap to be a regular person of sorts, Harry was flying. But royal watchers cautioned that the faster he went, the more eyes would be on him, and the closer the microscope on that blurry line between trading off his royal blood and simply being who he was—*made* of royal blood. Some, it seemed, were hellbent on criticizing the hard working duke. You cannot take the blue out of the veins, they said.

Daily Mirror royal editor Russell Myers pointed out, "There is the argument that if he is 'Prince Harry, the Duke of Sussex in all the published materials for [the firm], is that trading off the royal brand which they said they wouldn't do to uphold the values of The Queen?" he suggested. "So it is very debatable at the moment. People at the Palace will be watching this very, very closely."

Oh, do shut up.

In the end, the bullying allegations Buckingham Palace was so worried about before the Oprah interview, that *"investigation"* they were fast and furious on, apparently went nowhere. High-profile senior advisor Jason Knauf left his post with the British royal family rather abruptly in the months after the accusations were revealed. Some interesting questions about whether the bullying claims were made in good faith, and if they were entirely true, and if certain advisers threw them out simply as a distraction to do anything, *anything,* to preemptively discredit the Sussexes, can be found online.

For example, *Royally Us* podcast host Molly Mulshine posited, "It definitely makes me think Meghan may not be as guilty as they made out in this situation. If [Knauf] really felt confident about the allegations that he made, then why would you leave the job two months later? If you really felt like you had this important investigation to carry out, I just don't see why you would leave. I think there's a lot of intrigue here, something fishy is going on."

The suspicious smell made it all the way to Montecito, where perhaps Meghan cooked up a platter of her favorite fish tacos, which she loves to make by grilling peppers and onions and a few filets of flaky white fish seasoned with salt and pepper and a little lime, all folded into a warm corn tortilla, and perhaps she and Harry thought about why Knauf left his post as they enjoyed the delectable fishy feast.

The couple continued full-steam ahead with their lives. In April, Harry got to announce an exciting new project that was very close to his heart. Their first Netflix project would be a docuseries titled "Heart of Invictus," which will follow servicemembers from around the globe "who have suffered life-changing injuries or illnesses" as they prepare to compete in the Invictus Games in The Hague in 2022.

"Since the very first Invictus Games back in 2014, we knew that each competitor would contribute in their own exceptional way to a mosaic of resilience, determination, and resolve," the Duke of Sussex said in the press release. "This series will give communities around the world a window into the moving and uplifting stories of these competitors on their path to the Netherlands next year."

Netflix boss Ted Sarandos also put out a statement:

"The Duke and Duchess of Sussex and the Archewell Productions team are building an ambitious slate that reflects the values and causes they hold dear," he said. "From the moment I met them, it's been clear that the Invictus Games hold a very special place in their hearts, and I couldn't be happier that their first series for Netflix will showcase that for the world in a way never seen before."

That was early April, and one wonders if The Firm was feeling the need to take some of their own positive headlines. It seemed perhaps senior royals were scrambling to prove their usefulness to a public whose money they continued to use? For the first time ever, it was announced that same week, tourists would suddenly be allowed on the grounds of Buckingham Palace! Yep: It would be BYO cucumber sandwiches and Pimms. Lay a blanket a the feet of The Queen. You, too, would be able to partake in self-guided tours of the 39-acre gardens for the first time in the palace's history. You could hang outside the Queen's own house on her "sweeping lawns" from July to September.

There has long been a case made that British taxpayers do not need to be supporting this family. In fact, it is quite easy to knock down the favorite claim that "the royals bring in (insert huge number here) of pounds in tourist money!"

Guess what? It's a long-known fact that royal residences around the globe *do not need live royals in residence in order to bring in the cash.* The *properties and the history* bring in the tourists. Even in the UK. The unoccupied Hampton

Court Palace hosts staggering numbers of visitors, for example, and provides a raft of jobs for British subjects. But guess what? No *actual live royals* reside there. The country would do just fine with a Buckingham Palace free of Andrew, Charles, William or their consorts.

In any case, they were now opening up their meadows "carpeted with primroses and bluebells... flowering camellia, magnolia and azalea shrubs and tree" to icky commoners, said the Royal Collection Trust.

April got underway and Meghan and Harry were at home in Montecito, getting ready for summer, a new world with growing herd immunity, and the impending birth of their daughter. In the midst of that, they were finalizing deals left right and center. Meanwhile, speculation swirled about whether Harry would turn up to unveil Diana's statue alongside his brother.

In the wee hours of April 9, when Harry was deep in a slumber, a member of their security team woke him up. The U.S. Embassy had tried to reach Harry directly, but apparently his cell phone was on silent or he simply never heard it, according to reporting by TMZ. Desperate to reach the Prince, the Embassy staffer contacted the Santa Barbara Sheriffs Department to ask an officer could go to the Sussex estate. An officer rolled up to the estate's gates and from there, Harry was awakened and informed that, alas, the Royal family suffered a true loss that week as Prince Philip died that very morning.

At noon local time, the Royal Family Twitter account broke the news to the world: *It is with deep sorrow that Her*

Majesty The Queen has announced the death of her beloved husband, His Royal Highness The Prince Philip, Duke of Edinburgh. His Royal Highness passed away peacefully this morning at Windsor Castle.

Shortly after the announcement, the flag at Buckingham Palace was lowered to half-mast and flowers—daffodils, tulips, roses and lilies—were quickly laid by members of the public outside the palace as crowds gathered at Windsor Castle. That day, the Queen lost her husband of 73 years. The Duke of Edinburgh had been the longest-serving consort in British history.

The BBC's royal correspondent Nicholas Witchell said it was "a moment of real national sadness" and added Prince Philip had made "a huge contribution to the success of the Queen's reign," describing the duke as "utterly loyal in his belief in the importance of the role that the Queen was fulfilling—and in his duty to support her…It was the importance of the solidity of that relationship, of their marriage, that was so crucial to the success of her reign."

Early response was respectful and lauded his contribution to Britain, with syrupy tributes coming from Britain's elite, from Boris Johnson to BBC commentators and all in between.

Unsentimental types on social media immediately speculated about how long it would take for someone in power to blame Meghan for "killing" Philip, with one writing, "they're gonna say his cause of death was Meghan Markle."

The author Roxane Gay Tweeted, "Whew. The way the are gonna blame the Duchess of Sussesx. Smh. Jesus be a force field around her."

They were right—but they were too slow. It took minutes—*minutes*—after the announcement of his death for a major network to suggest some blame lay with Philip's heavily pregnant grand-daughter-in-law who lived 6,000-miles away.

Brian Kilmeade connected Philip's death of old age at 99 to the big Oprah interview. "If you factor in this, there are reports that he was enraged after the interview...here he is trying or recover, and then he gets hit with that."

Further, he said with great concern in his voice for poor Philip who very possibly was sent to his grave at the hands of a couple going about their business on the other side of the globe, "there's one thing that Piers Morgan was saying...is like really?...your grandfather's in the hospital. He's not doing well. Is this really the time you have to put out this interview? And evidently it definitely added to his stress."

Interestingly, there was no known suggestion that day by any media figures that Philip was pushed to the brink by his son Andrew's alleged pedophilia and human trafficking and the fact that he is connected to an epic web of crime and horrific damage to children via the late Jeffrey Epstein.

Before his grandfather was even buried, Prince Harry was back in the news, but not for anything he'd said or done. Speculation swirled about how he, Meghan and

Archie would handle the surrounding events for Philip's long goodbye.

While the world kept guessing, the Sussexes' plans were already firmly in place: Harry would go back alone.

The night before he left, Harry leaned on Meghan, took deep breaths, tried to get enough sleep, and steeled himself. He knew that going back to London would certainly trigger those same feelings of being trapped and hunted and pursued by photographers and tabloid reporters, and of course family relations at the time were rocky.

Harry has said he was "worried" and "afraid" about going. Meanwhile, it seemed like the entire world was speculating on exactly when he would go, how long he would stay, and who he would be seen talking to in public. He needed coping mechanisms to face it all, and he had some in his toolbox now thanks to regular therapy sessions. That, he said, "made it a lot easier. But the heart still pounds."

Apart from its focus on Harry, the coverage of the death was interesting in its handling of Philip's long-displayed racism. The Duke of Edinburgh, after all, had a long history of what his country's media liked to call "gaffes" but in actuality revealed some deep-seated racism he didn't bother to hide. Columbia University's Hamid Dabashi said it well in an opinion piece for Al Jazeera a few years before, pointing out a few of Philip's greatest hits including, "It looks as if it was put in by an Indian" while talking about a fixture at a factory in Scotland; or, when he asked an Aboriginal Australian while visiting their country,

"Still throwing spears?"; and "If you stay here much longer you'll all be slitty-eyed," something he said to British students while conducting an official royal engagement in China. He added, "Prince Philip—how shall we put it gently here—is a rank racist."

Which, again, is all so blatant and public that it would be little surprise if he'd been the one to talk in such brazenly racist terms about unborn Archie's skin color. No, if we were to be surprised by who said it, didn't it have to be someone who knew he had to hide it better than that?

The day after Philip's death, when the BBC was receiving record numbers of complaints for its wall-to-wall coverage of the royal loss (they even preempted favorite shows about gardening and the evening soap *East Enders*), the *Daily Mail* still could not help itself.

The editors splashed a massive headline across its front page blaring to the world that MEGHAN ISN'T COMING TO THE FUNERAL. Even for the tabloids, this focus on a woman who no longer used an HRH title and was far along in a geriatric pregnancy in the middle of a raging pandemic, seemed bizarrely obsessive.

Harry went alone. He was spotted leaving Montecito and heading to LAX for a scheduled flight back to Heathrow well in advance of his grandfather's April 17 burial. It was his first trip home since March 2020, and the first time he would be seeing his brother and father Prince Charles, who sources told the British media was "looking forward" to the reunion. The distractions were many. First, the face-to-face meeting they would eventually have was billed around the world as a tense showdown between two estranged brothers who had grown up as two peas in a pod.

Newspapers, television and social media were flooded with predictions: Would they put on a show of unity? Would they display true warmth and reconciliation in the face of the death of the family patriarch? Or would the rift prove to be too wide to traverse, especially so publically?

Meghan sat at home, quietly taking care of herself, as Harry—according to early reports—hunkered down for a brief period to quarantine at his old bolt hole, Nottingham Cottage, only feet from where Will, Kate and the kids live in Central London's Kensington Palace. Soon it became clear he was at Frogmore Cottage, the home he and Meghan ordered to be renovated (they repaid the cost of that), and then loaned to Eugenie and her new husband.

No one heard from the younger royals until that Monday, when both Harry and William released written tributes to the grandfather they shared. If William was attempting to sound regal, it came off as stiff, stilted and even a bit dull, especially when compared to Harry's heartfelt and cheeky sendoff. Furthermore, whatever way writers and royal watchers leaned on the royal rift, all corners seemed to agree that William had proffered a dig at Harry in his own statement.

From Sussex Squaddies on Twitter to friend-of-the-royals and writer Richard Kay, it was pointed out that this was a not-so-subtle jab at Harry's newfound freedom. Wrote Kay… "was there one icy barb directed at his brother [in William's statement]? 'Catherine and I,' he wrote, 'will continue to do what he would have wanted and will support the Queen in the years ahead. I will miss my grandpa, but I know he would want us to get on with the job.'" Kay himself concluded that, "Two brothers, two very different ways of marking their grandfather's life, but no sign of any healing comments to mend a heart-breaking rift."

Harry showed a playful way with words, speaking in vivid, snappy imagery: "He was authentically himself, with a seriously sharp wit, and could hold the attention of any room due to his charm—and also because you never knew what he might say next," he said in the statement through his Archewell Foundation.

"He will be remembered as the longest reigning consort to the Monarch, a decorated serviceman, a Prince and a Duke. But to me, like many of you who have lost a loved one or grandparent over the pain of this past year, he was my grandpa: master of the barbecue, legend of banter, and cheeky right 'til the end," Harry continued. "He has been a rock for Her Majesty The Queen with unparalleled devotion, by her side for 73 years of marriage, and while I could go on, I know that right now he would say to all of us, beer in hand, 'Oh do get on with it!' So, on that note, Grandpa, thank you for your service, your dedication to Granny, and for always being yourself. You will be sorely missed, but always remembered—by the nation and the world. Meghan, Archie, and I (as well as your future great-granddaughter) will always hold a special place for you in our hearts."

He signed off with the words many fans around the world scrambled to research the meaning of: "Per Mare, Per Terram," which is Latin for "By Sea, by Land."

By Tuesday, papers were reporting Harry was *actually* quarantining for COVID-19 at Frogmore Cottage in Windsor where he last lived with Meghan before decamping to North America, which is interesting because his cousin lived there. Meanwhile, William and Kate were said to be relaxing at Anmer Hall in Norfolk while their three children had their spring holidays.

The brothers were far apart both in every way, and a reunion before the funeral seemed unlikely.

There didn't have to be any other reason for Meghan to stay home other than her and her baby's health, but still the media brought in family politics. "Meghan said her main concern right now is supporting Harry. She said she left it up to him as to whether or not she would attend the funeral," DailyMail.com reported, quoting "an insider with close ties to Meghan Markle." Continued this "insider," "Meghan said it's during these times when family should come together, put their differences aside and unite as one. She said this is what Prince Philip would want and that she's willing to forgive and move forward," they said.

The anonymous assertion that Meghan was "letting" Harry go alone and that the decision for her to stay home was for anything other than health and safety was dubious, because Meghan already had a firm, understandable and very personal reason for not going. The exact factors were between her and her doctor. But once again, while taking care of herself at home tucked in the Santa Inez mountain range with Archie and soon-to-be-born Baby Girl Sussex and letting the United Kingdom mourn their longtime consort to their beloved Queen without distractions from her, people still talked.

One offended host on Australian television shook her head at the anonymous claim that Meghan stayed home so as not to be a distraction on the day of the funeral, saying it "just really gets my goat. That just makes me so angry." The host added that the quotes about Meghan staying home not to draw attention to herself were fair—but she still wasn't happy with the duchess.

"She's right," the woman said. "If she had gone, there would have been a lot of attention on her…just go with the palace line for once…just shut up. Pretend [health reasons were] what it was and then we can all continue on."

The host of the Sunrise show didn't clarify for her audience that Meghan hadn't said a word about it, or that an unnamed "friend" of a reporter for the sister publication Meghan has sued had written those words.

When the day for the funeral finally came on a brisk spring Saturday, most of the coverage focused on the Queen. But there were the inevitable style shout-outs and focus on the women and how they looked and what they wore, especially Kate in her jewels and neat chignon.

And so Harry went, and walked near his brother, but not next to him. There was a buffer deliberately inserted between them. It was first believed the courtiers (or Charles or the Queen as the case may be) saw fit to separate the brothers by inserting a barrier in the form of their cousin Peter Phillips. But a report soon emerged from the Kensington-Palace-friendly *Mail on Sunday* newspaper that Prince William went out of his way to ask that he not have to walk next to Harry. Furthermore, it was claimed senior royals including his aunt and uncle Princess Anne and Prince Edward refused to even acknowledge Harry at all, a snub that was just one element among "a great deal of frostiness" he faced on his trip back home.

As the procession began, William and Harry gave the British media very little to pick apart, so the press pulled out some of their favorite column-inch-packers: the body language expert and the lip reader. Without actual information about what the brothers were thinking or how they'd been interacting before their walk in the glare of the public gaze, they used "experts" to guess.

When the service was over, William and Harry were seen interacting in a usual way that families do—calmly and respectfully as they chatted on their way out of the chapel. This very basic and unremarkable moment "signals a bright future for the reportedly feuding siblings," said one expert. "In a well-coordinated but also relatively natural-looking moment, Harry walked up behind William and Kate to then join them, walking between them and chatting to them both."

People magazine's source offered this analysis: "The procession choreography, in retrospect, was a mistake," historian Robert Lacey, author of the bestselling biography *Battle of Brothers*, said. "As we saw, they could have walked side-by-side quite happily after all. What pleased me afterward was that it all seemed so totally natural, and they drifted to each other like the old days."

But the oddest storyline to dominate the day that was meant to be about celebrating the life of man who died at 99 was the made-up narrative that Kate was now the family "peacemaker." Without Meghan there, Kate, now seeming like a blank slate on which the world could write whatever it wanted, was pictured being personable and chatty with Harry, in stark contrast to the frigid treatment on show at the foursome's last encounter in the Abbey many months before.

Googling "Kate" and "peacemaker" brings up enough headlines and definitive pronouncements that one wonders if she should be up for a Nobel Peace prize. Of course, this is not her fault. The media continues to gaze up on the empty canvas she offers up and paint on it whatever suits them. (Note, too, that Kate's blank canvas is also not entirely her fault—her role is to sit still and look pretty, and she does it well, and she is rewarded for it).

Wrote one paper, "After Saturday's emotional funeral William and Harry took 'baby steps' towards healing their relationship after they walked back to Windsor Castle from St George's Chapel together after being pushed together by peacemaker Kate, the Duchess of Cambridge."

London News Today was one of many to put forward that "Prince Phillip's funeral reveals that the future of the royal family is safe—with Kate as a new rock." She is, in fact, the Queen's new "rock," they said. Which was an absurd assertion on its face, but also in light of the fact it was based solely on some images from the procession in which the three younger royals were not punching each other's faces in.

While Harry was in town, in a desperate attempt to craft a saleable story, the British media put out this jumbled narrative. William and Harry were talking—but Charles wasn't involved. Harry wrote Charles a "heartfelt letter"—or the pair remained on icy terms. Again, Meghan, at home saying nothing, was endlessly pulled in as a character in a story about a funeral.

Later there was apparently a face-to-face meeting within the grounds of the castle between the brothers and their father Prince Charles, "but, in an unprecedented development that lays bare the depth of their rift, Charles and William preferred to meet with Harry together so that nobody's words could be misconstrued afterwards, MailOnline's Dan Wootton revealed."

The journalists tried to guess when Harry would go back to California, with many suggesting if he didn't stay alone in town for his grandmother's birthday, it would constitute "rushing" back. He stayed for two days after the funeral, then went back to his heavily pregnant wife and young son.

Wrote one smitten man on Twitter next to a photo of Meghan: "If I was married to her, I'd rush home too."

He returned on April 19.

Not only did he miss the Queen's birthday, reported the Dailymail.com, but he left "with the Windsors' family row unresolved after meeting only once with his father and Prince William following the Duke of Edinburgh's funeral."

His driver picked him up from LAX and pulled up to the gate Sussexes' Montecito home that afternoon, and it felt like an eternity to get through the security gate and travel the private road up to their estate. There, Meghan and Archie were waiting with big hugs and a warm welcome as Archie chattered about his time holding down the fort while daddy was back in England, playing with the dogs and playing pretend in his kid-sized house.

Meantime, the Queen spent a quiet day with select members of her family—but it is understood that neither Prince Charles nor Prince William joined her, though that was barely a footnote while interestingly Harry was the subject of many headlines pointing out that he wouldn't be with the Queen. There has never been an indication or suggestion that the Queen had requested he be there or was particularly concerned if her grandson was in residence on the day. It was a different kind of birthday for the oldest reigning monarch on many fronts, as the traditional fanfare such as official family photos or gun salutes or birthday because Queen Elizabeth was in a period of mourning.

10

How dare they be happy

Not long after Harry reunited with his family, Meghan took a trip to L.A. with Archie. Doria lives there, so Meghan was making her trip down to the big city while she still could, before she was due and went on maternity leave. She was caught there by the ubiquitous feral paparazzi pack, and they caught a lovely new shot of Archie, who now looks so much like his father that a fan joked on social media that the child "stole his whole face."

Meghan had her hands full and looked gorgeous as ever, even in her mask, and had the glow of a woman soon to have a daughter to (possibly) complete her family. Everything was well.

Just kidding.

The internet immediately pounced with various negative responses from critiques of the way she was holding Archie "on her bump," to claiming she set up the paparazzi shot in order to release it at the same time as Kate and William released a new photo of youngest son Louis. The *International Business Times* helpfully rounded it up and headlined it "Meghan Markle Propping Archie Up On Baby Bump Sparks Concern On Twitter."

And still Meghan and Harry didn't engage or respond. "Genuinely pregnant women carry their toddlers on their hip, the child's legs under the bump. #MeghanMarkle balances 'Archie' on top of her bump, knees digging into it," a second user sneered. "How is a pregnant woman able to carry that weight over her stomach," another asked.

Fans shot back to the bitter diatribes. "Seriously? If you know anyone or have had children close together you should know that it's perfectly normal to hold you're toddler/baby while pregnant!" Shouted back a fellow mom.

The world didn't know that Meghan had another project up her sleeve. She'd been working on it since her and Harry's days in Windsor, where the idea had germinated with a few sweet, simple scenes she'd seen on Father's Day of 2018. From there she brought her vision to completion.

The announcement was made in May of 2021 that Meghan, the Duchess of Sussex, had done something so harmful, so controversial, and so calculated that it almost defied belief: *She wrote a children's book*. It's true—she secured a publisher and put out a book full of her own thoughts, one illustrated with colorful pictures aimed at *innocent children* by Caldecott-winning artist Christian Robinson. *The Bench*, the world learned, would tell the story of the bonds between fathers and sons as described by their mothers.

The British media was not going to let her get away with it. The *Telegraph* newspaper was particularly concerned: "Meghan Markle's fun-free children's book may put an entire generation off reading," screamed one headline. The deck beneath it explained further that, "Yes, parents will buy it. But the intended audience for the Duchess of Sussex's literary debut prefers silliness and being scared to sermons."

And how. Images from *The Bench* released pre-publication were truly off-putting: One showed a boy overcome with happiness by the homecoming of his military father, and another revealed a Black child napping sweetly on his father's chest, cuddling a stuffed giraffe. The *nerve.*

Thankfully, there was an antidote at the ready to these brutal images. In a sweeping red coat that rather resembled a ball gown, Kate Middleton, whose name is also on a book, went out on a deserted road, knelt, facing away from the camera, and "hid" a few copies of said book.

Plastered across the front of the *Daily Mail* along with those pictures was a screaming headline: "EAT YOUR HEART OUT, MEGHAN."

Meghan tried her best to explain her own book, but her continued inflammatory rhetoric only exacerbated things. "*The Bench* started as a poem I wrote for my husband on Father's Day, the month after Archie was born," the Duchess of Sussex desperately claimed. "That poem became this story."

As life went on and The Bench went on pre-sale, Meghan continued her selfish undertakings despite the backlash to her annoying book. On May 8, the world saw a heavily pregnant duchess "showing off" her bump (guess whose headline that was?) while talking about the need for COVID-19 vaccination equality around the world.

In a recorded speech for Global Citizen's Vax Live, an event attended by a fully vaccinated audience of frontline workers at SoFi Stadium in Los Angeles, Meghan talked about how vital gender equity is, and pointed out that women have been disproportionately affected by COVID-19. She also shared thoughts on her baby girl: "My husband and I are thrilled to soon be welcoming a daughter. It's a feeling of joy we share with millions of other families around the world. When we think of her, we think of all the other families around the globe who must be given the ability and support to lead us forward."

Her baby was due in a matter of weeks. Meghan remained in Montecito, blissed out in that way many expecting women are who are safe, surrounded by loved ones and have excellent health care, with a constant joy tempered by bouts of discomfort, some trouble sleeping, and a mind swimming with to-do lists and possibilities of what lay ahead.

Harry continued stepping out, further charming a nation that had already embraced and welcomed him. He spoke utterly, charmingly frankly with Dax Shepard and Monica Padman on their Armchair Expert podcast. Harry, who helped produce an AppleTV+ mental-health related docuseries with Oprah and who had launched the UK's Head's Together campaign with William and Kate (with the aim of joining mental health charities together), revealed some of his deepest feelings and childhood memories. He spoke openly about his late mother, a beloved and controversial figure in his life (sound familiar?). Diana, Princess of Wales, died young in a Paris car crash in 1997 when Harry was twelve. "The massive immense impact that she had on us in the short time she was around was huge, because all she wanted to do was make sure we had as normal a life as possible," Harry recalled of his and William's childhood.

Another theme Harry has begun reflecting on publicly since meeting his wife is the idea of inheritance. He inherited money, extreme risk to his physical being, a title, and family trauma. It's time, he's said, to break at least one of those cycles.

"I don't think we should be pointing the finger or blaming anybody, but certainly when it comes to parenting, if I've experienced some form of pain or suffering because of the pain or suffering that perhaps my father or my parents had suffered, I'm going to make sure I break that cycle so that I don't pass it on, basically.

It's a lot of genetic pain and suffering that gets passed on anyway so we as parents should be doing the most we can to try and say, 'You know what, that happened to me, I'm going to make sure that doesn't happen to you.'"

The podcast is a great listen, and basic transcripts can also be found online. Some of the most revelatory discussions were about coming to terms with the attacks he and Meghan have faced.

"Hatred is a form of projection—we're not born to hate people," Harry shared. "It manifests itself over a period of time and it comes from a place of unresolved pain. Ultimately, there's a source for it. There's a reason you want to hate somebody else. When it comes to trolling on social media I take a moment to look at it and say, okay, this is how it's making me feel, but I flip it and say, okay, how's your day going? What happened to you? And actually have some compassion for them. Which is hard when you're on the receiving end of some vile, toxic abuse; but I try and think, what's your goal? What made you come at me?"

On that same day, almost a full year after he'd first driven through the gates of his new home in Montecito, he revealed it had been a necessary move that brought more happiness than he thought possible:

"Living [in Santa Barbara] now I can actually lift my head and I feel different, my shoulders have dropped, so have [Meghan's], you can walk around feeling a little bit more free, I can take Archie on the back of my bicycle, I would never have had the chance to do that" back in the UK.

Actor Dax Shepard could barely contain himself after the interview. He admitted he'd been surprised by a well-known fact about his new royal pal:. "Prince Harry. My Man flew an Apache in Afghanistan; one of a dozen surprises that left me respecting this intellectual, thoughtful human being. And watching @mlpadman react to him was once in a life time," Dax Tweeted.

Right on cue, replies from detractors came fast and furious, with smart-sounding statements proclaiming Harry never actually flew Apaches. Some seemed like they were not OK, including Smartiepants73: "He never flew an Apache helicopter! He flew in one!"

Kristi Walker replied calmly on Twitter, "He is a fully qualified Apache pilot. Of course he had protection and other privileges most military pilots don't have but to his credit he absolutely did the work. His army mates consistently defend him and speak of his intellect and hard work and that says a lot about him."

Kristi Walker was correct. The facts are this: Harry qualified as an Apache commander (source: BBC News and literally everywhere else if you do the basic research) and yes, he *flew* them.

All along, the Sussexes had been in talks with sponsors, business, creatives and more, and it was hard work. They'd committed to a life of self-sufficiency instead of living off the government or the generational wealth that originally came from conquering and claiming land and assets that may or may not have involved ill-gotten gains in the olden days.

Harry did have some of his own money, including his inheritance from his mother, but it wasn't going to be enough to pay for the extreme security costs for his family in perpetuity.

And so when it came time to announce a new money-making deal, Meghan braced herself once again. Feeling a bit heavy and sluggish so late in her pregnancy, she centered herself in Montecito and made a point of taking time to breathe and practice her beloved yoga. Finally, they let the announcement out: They'd be working with Archewell in a partnership with Procter & Gamble (the same company she'd called out for a sexist ad 28 years before) on a long-term initiative. It will "focus on gender equality, more inclusive online spaces, and resilience and impact through sport."

The backlash was swift. She didn't bother reading about it, because Meghan had come to know that it wasn't her or Harry's problem. It was the problem of the people fuming about something that really didn't affect them.

"Royal expert" Angela Levin told *The Sun* that "It's all about telling everybody else what to do and not...doing it [yourself]." She added, "it's all wishy washy as usual. There's a fog around a lot of what they do and I think this is another foggy deal.

[Meghan] has sort of said ludicrous things like 'want to elevate the voice of adolescents and girls to make sure their point of view and lived experiences are heard at the table where decisions are made.' But all that talk "doesn't make sense."

Even so far down the line with the Oprah interview in the rearview mirror and Meghan and Harry sailing through their new life without asking for a thing from anyone, the hypocrisy still flew. The Sussexes were criticized for working with a company with a "checkered past." But how hard could it have been for *The Sun* newspaper to figure out the Queen herself has a long collaboration with that very same company? Yet Meghan and Harry have to worry about P&G's "checkered past."

You know who else deals with that company? Will and Kate. Wrote Ad Age around their 2011 wedding, "Procter & Gamble, the latest marketer to succumb to royal wedding fever, is developing a special-edition plastic bottle of its best-selling dishwashing detergent, Fairy Liquid, to commemorate the wedding of Prince William to Kate Middleton on April 29. The consumer goods giant already has a Royal Warrant for the Fairy Liquid brand, which is known as Dreft outside the U.K. The regular bottles carry the queen's coat of arms and the words "By Appointment to Her Majesty the Queen. Manufacturers of Soap and Detergents." (The royal family lets its favorite product suppliers promote themselves as Royal Warrant holders.)

At the time, P&G said in a statement: "We know how much public excitement is already building and we are thrilled to have Fairy involved."

That spring, Harry blossomed away from the family he was born into. The more he steered the conversation and told his story in his own words, the more alarmed the British media became. He signaled he was now in control of his own narrative. Harry didn't always please everyone, but he wasn't apologizing—even when some of his true fans cringed a bit when he made a misstep speaking about freedom of speech, which is protected by the United States

Constitution's First Amendment. Still, some pointed out he admitted he didn't fully understand it yet and was simply sharing his learning process. "I've got so much I want to say about the First Amendment as I sort of understand it, but it is bonkers," he said on Dax Shepard's podcast.

By their third wedding anniversary in late May, the couple was too busy preparing for their second child's arrival to bother worrying about the small things. With the pandemic still raging and slamming India with a humanitarian emergency of frightening proportions, the Sussexes didn't come out with a new photo of Archie or an unseen romantic shot of them. Instead, they chose that day to say they would redouble their efforts working in partnership with superhero chef José Andrés and his disaster relief nonprofit World Central Kitchen.

"In support of India, Archewell Foundation and World Central Kitchen are focusing on the long-term needs of local communities," read the Archewell statement. "The Mumbai location will be the third in a series of four Community Relief Centers that our organizations have committed to develop in regions of the world disproportionately affected by natural disaster."

Clearly, the Sussexes had no time for pettiness that spring. On the day of their third anniversary Meghan was at home in Montecito getting ready for a cozy night with her husband when she learned Buckingham Palace announced their friend Princess Beatrice was expecting her first child, she had to smile; whether it was a calculated move or not, she was genuinely happy for Bea. Harry and

Meghan shrugged it off and didn't think too much of it either way.

While many viewed the announcement's timing as a dig at Harry and Meghan, who had announced she was pregnant with Archie on Beatrice's sister Eugenie's wedding day back in October 2018, one source says Meghan and Harry sent heartfelt and private congratulations to Beatrice and her husband.

Meanwhile back in the UK, William was stepping out for public events in earnest, letting people know he was still working and at least taking a stab at earning his keep.

The headlines in England were largely pro-monarchy, and William and Kate talked about mental health and said if you feel bad, "talk about it." But when his brother shared his pain it wasn't OK.

Also that season, William, who did not share when or for how long he had COVID, shared a photo of himself allegedly receiving a shot he said was a vaccine. Some wondered if it was plausible the future king had waited so long for such vital protection, but the photo went wide nonetheless and gave Will a bump of goodwill he badly needed. His bicep on show was a thirst trap, some said.

That part of the family was more distant than ever, but Harry was still thriving. The baby was coming anytime now, the guest house was designed and decked out to a T. Grandma Doria was a regular visitor and planning to take time off to move into the unit to help in those first weeks of baby girl Sussex's life.

With COVID slipping away in California as vaccinations increased, Meghan felt calmer about the upcoming birth; it felt like the dangerous pandemic had abated enough to make the experience an amazing and very personal one. It has long been believed by those who know her that she had wanted a home birth. (Side note: Look for Meghan to one day take up the cause of eliminating the term "geriatric pregnancy" altogether in this country, say sources. An extremely healthy woman in her thirties called "geriatric" is, to many women, an unnecessarily loaded and even insulting label, even if it's technically medically correct; some believe Meghan also balked at it).

Meghan spent the long Memorial Day weekend ready to drop, feeling like something *had* to happen soon. Harry and the family took some quiet moments to think about and acknowledge all those who had lost their lives or their loved ones in the military, and both prepared for their upcoming leave from working by taking care of last-minute details and ensuring all was ready for Baby Girl Sussex.

On June 4, 1996, Princess Diana, Harry's mother and Archie's grandmother, visited Northwestern University during a two-day tour of the Chicago, Illinois area. She charmed everyone she met during that fundraising trip, and left an indelible mark.

Exactly twenty-five years later, on June 4, 2021, Northwestern graduate Meghan Markle gave birth to Diana's granddaughter. That incredible coincidence made the moment all the more special.

Despite persistent rumors and claims that Meghan had always wanted to give birth at home, Lili, like big brother Archie, was born in a hospital. In the wee hours, Meghan knew the baby was coming and everyone scrambled. She stepped calmly into the Land Rover with Harry in tow with the overnight bag, and off they went to Santa Barbara Cottage Hospital, where an American princess was born on U.S. soil, eighth in line for the British throne—unprecedented.

The first person they called was Her Majesty The Queen. What happened after Harry dialed her up was publicly disputed and would spark an international outcry, lead to high-profile firings and threats of legal action, and cast a shadow over the beginning of a beautiful new life.

But first came the official announcement: "It is with great joy that Prince Harry and Meghan, The Duke and Duchess of Sussex, welcome their daughter, Lilibet 'Lili' Diana Mountbatten-Windsor, to the world," said a spokesperson on June 6, a full two days after the birth. "Both mother and child are healthy and well, and settling in at home…The Duke and Duchess thank you for your warm wishes and prayers as they enjoy this special time as a family.

"Lili is named after her great-grandmother, Her Majesty The Queen, whose family nickname is Lilibet. Her middle name, Diana, was chosen to honor her beloved late grandmother, The Princess of Wales. The Duke and Duchess thank you for your warm wishes and prayers as they enjoy this special time as a family." at Santa Barbara Cottage Hospital."

Apart from the baby's name, which delighted but did not shock many people—"Diana" is always batted around when a new British royal baby is on the way—the most remarkable outcome of the entire experience was the lack of media leaks. Meghan gave birth Friday. The press release went out Sunday. The media went mad trumpeting the news around the globe.

Keen royal watchers shook their heads with amazed respect: Now that the Sussexes were in America, no one was betraying them. Wrote one Sussex fan on Twitter, "Not one California media outlet leak. Not one friend leak. Not one staff leak. Not one leak. Speaks volumes about where all leaks were coming from over the years #UK!"

Popular former blogger Love, Lola explained why that might be: "This is part of what Prince Harry was referring to when he discussed privacy," she Tweeted. "When they were at the Palace, the call was coming from inside the house. Now they get to share what they want on their own terms."

Next came a personal note from the couple: "She is more than we could have ever imagined, and we remain grateful for the love and prayers we've felt from across the globe," Harry and Meghan said. "Thank you for your continued kindness and support during this very special time for our family."

And finally, the Sussexes could relax and bask in well wishes and love pouring out from every corner. They knew that finally, once and for all, they had done something so pure that no one could criticize them. A new baby was a blessing.

Right?

Just kidding.

Many with a platform within the British media, as well as angry internet strangers, seemed to feel that a little tiny baby merited an attack from all sides. Obviously, this baby had been one of the more controversial infants born in recent times. Right out of the womb, she was already acting up. Something had to be done to make sure her first few days of life were tinged with ugliness.

Columnist Julie Burchill, a longtime public figure in the UK and noted anti-trans writer who's called trans women "dicks in chicks' clothing," stepped up. Lilbet Diana's name was sparking conversation the world over, and Burchill joined in: "What a missed opportunity! They could have called it Georgina Floydina!" she Tweeted, referring to the brutal murder of George Floyd by a police officer in Minneapolis. Royal watchers and social media commentators let that sink in, and in the meantime…

Many loud angry people were not happy that the couple had chosen "Lilibet," a "very personal" childhood nickname for granny Elizabeth, and made their objections quite clear. The BBC reported that Queen Elizabeth was "never asked" about her grandson's decision to name his second child after her, adding fuel to the anti-Lilibet fire.

The Sussexes' team shot back swiftly: "The Duke spoke with his family in advance of the announcement, in fact his grandmother was the first family member he called. During that conversation, he shared their hope of naming their daughter Lilibet in her honor." The spokesperson added, "Had she not been supportive, they would not have used the name."

As is always the case, words matter. And the ones put out by anonymous palace sources and by the Sussexes themselves were parsed within an inch of their lives. The use of the phrase "shared their hope" is not the same as asking permission, critics said. Being "supportive" is not the same as "giving permission," they pointed out. The dispute raged in the press and on social media, with many Sussex fans shaking their virtual heads: "What's the Palace's end game?" posited one. "It's not like they're going to change her name. Lilibet is here to stay."

A friend of the Sussexes told *People* magazine that Harry introduced Lili to the queen over a video call, but that too was disputed across the pond. Wrote the *Mail on Sunday* the following week, "there was further irritation at the Palace when friends of Harry and Meghan suggested to US journalists that the Queen had been introduced to Lilibet over a video call. The insider last night denied that, stating, 'No video call has taken place', adding: 'Friends of the Sussexes appear to have given misleading briefings to journalists about what the Queen had said and that took the whole thing over the edge. The Palace couldn't deny the story that this was a mistruth.'"

Yet as backward as the UK was proving to still be, as resistant as the nation as a whole was to being dragged kicking and screaming into the twenty-first century for an honest discussion about race and racism within their borders, something finally gave in relation to press treatment of Meghan.

Julie Burchill, who'd Tweeted that horrifically hurtful sentiment, was widely condemned for the "racist" remark, as well as for calling Lilibet "it." Finally, she was "sacked" by conservative broadsheet newspaper *The Telegraph*. Which was great, but some suggested she wasn't necessarily let go because of her *racism*, but because her racist Tweet attracted so much *attention*, amplified as it was a million-fold by a disgusted international audience who'd spent months grieving for George Floyd. (The United States is in the midst of its own reckoning with a racist history and culture, but right at that moment, the British media and the people supporting anti-Meghan sentiment were a far more vocal crowd).

After all, Burchill had been called out before in Britain—she'd paid substantial damages to settle a libel and harassment lawsuit, and when she lost, she wrote in a statement that the posts at issue had "included racist and misogynist comments" and "played into Islamophobic tropes."

That news didn't make more than a ripple across the pond.

Then, she remained as a *Telegraph* columnist.

This time, with a million eyes on her disgusting words, she was toast.

When Lili was a week old, NBC's Andrea Mitchell, an American journalist covering Kate Middleton and First Lady Dr. Jill Biden at a G7 event in Cornwall, probed the princess for any kind words she might have for her brother-and-sister-in-laws' new bundle of joy.

Tight grin plastered on, Kate replied vaguely, "I wish her all the very best, I can't wait to meet her because we haven't met her yet so hopefully that will be soon."

Though said through a smile, it came off as a chilly reply to the birth of a dear new life. RFM, a royal-watching Twitter account, almost instantly responded, "wish her the best??? Is she being let go from work? Like wtf lol also the US press is the best. They caught her out for trying to make it seem OK. It's not OK." Added Sussex fan Teambreeze, "It sounded like she was talking about a stranger not her sister-in-law I find that to be so cold."

Indeed, Mitchell pushed Kate and asked if there had been any video calls between the Cambridges and the Sussexes to introduce Lili, and Kate—perhaps ill-advisedly—answered the question. She admitted, "No, I haven't."

This bombshell that the two families, with two brothers tied together in a historically special way, *had not even spoken since the birth of a new princess* was reported around the world almost in real-time. Social media went wild. Twitter account royal whispers predicted Kate's husband would be wincing and planning to read his wife the riot act for revealing the information that Friday: "William will be incandescent with rage," they Tweeted. (It should be noted that this phrase has become a meme of sorts due to melodramatic palace leaks in the years since Harry met Meghan, in which anonymous sources report how angry William was about everything and routinely referring to him as "incandescent with rage").

And with that, the Britain-based side of the family sprung a leak that seemed to flow directly from Kate and Carole Middleton's camp. Kate's narrative had long included the claim that she and Harry were as close as a SIL and BIL could be, but whether that was the truth was never entirely clear. So, the day after Kate admitted she hadn't ever seen Harry's new child, a leak claimed that of course there had been a personal text message between the Duchess of Cambridge and the Duke of Sussex.

Sure, Jan, wrote one fierce Meghan supporter on Twitter: "That's why she put out the info about a text," wrote the Sussex fan known as Pagan Trelawney (a name that might sound familiar to fans of the book *Lace*). "It's hard to portray yourself as close to a person and a peacemaker if you haven't even FaceTimed a week after they had a baby. It reveals a lot about their relationship with you. It's definitely not closeness & definitely not trust."

For the few days before that, not much was heard from the Sussexes as they hunkered down with their family and got to know their daughter. It seems likely they were concocting plans to visit a homeless shelter to bring more attention to themselves, which is usually their only motivation, or perhaps hiring kids to organize next-level Rampant Avocado Production™. Maybe they were thinking of having another child just so they could name them some-thing that would make the royal family back in Britain Incandescent With Rage™. Who knows.

We do know that Meghan never stopped her gestures big and small, keeping up with her thank-you notes for all the gifts and cards coming in for Lilibet. She and Harry bathed in those and trusted their team to buffer them from the ugliness outside. They were briefed on big news that might need legal intervention, but all else was kept away from the pair who were determined to take proper mater-nity and paternity leave.

In the days after Lilibet's birth a recovering Meghan spent quiet time while the baby slept to reach out to those who'd connected with her. She wrote back to one fan and encouraged her to keep pursuing success even when things got heard. "Your good heart will guide you," Meghan wrote in her elegant cursive, and added a p.s. at the end to her fan's dog from her own, Guy and Pula.

Shortly before this very biography went to the printing presses, the New York *Times* bestseller list came out. Under Children's Picture Books, Meghan's book *The Bench* sat as the new #1 atop the list.

Considering days earlier tabloids had run headlines pronouncing (wrongly) that the book bombed out of the gate (receipts: "A real page-squirmer: Markle's new kids book fails remarkably." – The New York *Post*), it was now near-impossible to claim the media didn't target Meghan. They didn't care if they were wrong. They just wanted to get their digs in.

Meghan was smiling all the way to No. 1.

11

At the Gates of Bliss

July 2021

Exactly a year after Harry idled the SUV at the gates to their new Montecito home that represented so much hope and promise, all of it had come true. Their lives overflowing with love and possibility, with dramatic natural beauty surrounding them, the family of four greeted the summer of 2021 with hope in their eyes and love in their hearts.

"They are excited to see it all come together. It's what they have always dreamed of doing together," a friend of the couple told *People* magazine of their life in Montecito.

Harry would run with Archie in the sand, his little footprints disappearing in the surf, Meghan following with Lilibet warm on her chest in a baby carrier. As summer and Santa Barbara's beaches filled up with humanity once again unleashed with the beginnings of herd immunity and the easing of social distancing, the family of four remains in a paradise of their own making, a house they bought together with their own money, no restrictions on who they can lend their help to or when.

As Meghan bonds with her infant daughter in her airy nursery, sun pouring through the windows like angels riding on sunbeams, and whispers the words she repeated to herself when she was a struggling actress, the same ones her mother whispered to her, grasping Lili's little feet and touching them gently together, she smiles down at her daughter: *You are enough.*

Indeed, the family has let the world know they are enough, and as they continue to live their new independent lives, we will see it unfold in the coming years, with every likelihood of sweeping success despite the same pushback from a media and online trolls who find their success somehow disturbing. But now there is one huge difference: *now* they can deal with it however they see fit, and they will do it, as always, together.

Or…*wait* a minute. Is this a performance? Is the happy family image all a ruse to cover up sinister plans even *worse* than their Rampant Avocado Production™ scheme?

Sources tell us that hours later on that same night, with baby Lilibet safely tucked in her bed, Meghan headed downstairs, grabbed a basket, and padded outside to harvest more avocados from the grove in her backyard under the eerie light of a full moon, cackling evilly as she went, while Harry prepared the toast inside.

Just kidding.

All's well that ends well.

For now….

Author's Note

This biography recounts the history of Meghan and Harry and their relationship to the palace by presenting claims, quotes and legal documents put out by the couple *and* by the palace. For anything in dispute, both sides are included.

As this book is categorized as narrative nonfiction, some literary license has been taken to illustrate Harry and Megan's story and to illustrate the circumstances around facts, quotes and things the family themselves have shared.

And finally, because some of what has been said in the years is ludicrously absurd, there is some satire included.

Courtney Hargrove, author

June 29, 2021

Next in the series from One Moment Books…

Harry & Meghan, Vol. 2: Coming in 2022. Collect them all!

Printed in Great Britain
by Amazon